THE POWER OF DARKNESS

D1617520

First published in 1989 by Absolute Classics, an imprint of
Absolute Press, 14 Widcombe Crescent, Bath, England

© Anthony Clark

Series Editor: Giles Croft

Cover and text design: Ian Middleton

Photoset and printed by WBC Print, Bristol
Bound by W.H. Ware & Son, Clevedon

ISBN 0 948230 20 7

THE POWER OF DARKNESS
or
'If a claw is caught, the bird is lost.'

Leo Tolstoy

Translated and Adapted by Anthony Clark

But I say unto you, that whosoever looketh on a woman to lust after her
hath committed adultery with her already in his heart.
And if thy right eye offend thee, pluck it out, and cast it from thee:
for it is profitable for thee that one of thy members should perish, and
not that thy whole body should be cast into hell.

(Matthew V, verses 28-29)

a b s o l u t e   c l a s s i c s

INTRODUCTION

In 1879 Tolstoy, who came from a distinguished wealthy Russian aristocratic family, experienced a religious conversion, that transformed his thinking and behaviour. It led him to assimilate his life to that of a peasant.

Tolstoy's religious ideals are reflected in his later novels and in all his plays.

Tolstoy may have honoured the superior wisdom of the peasants, and exhorted people, particularly intellectuals, to copy their ways of life, but he could not help but be overcome with aristocratic revulsion at the physical and moral filth in which these primitive beings lived. Philosophically, he may have praised the Russian peasant, but artistically he draws him with absolute realistic veracity.

THE POWER OF DARKNESS was inspired by an actual occurence. On 18 January 1880, in a village in the district of Tula, a peasant, Koloskov, confessed to the assembled guests at his stepdaughter's wedding, that he had murdered a child she had borne him, and afterwards attempted to kill his own six year old daughter.

In 1886, Tolstoy develops this incident into a compelling drama that focuses on the cumulative effects of sinning. One sin leads to another with terrifying logic. The characters' lives grow more and more wretched.

Tolstoy wrote the play in the hopes that it might be performed by peasants to peasants, on *balagans* (open-air trestle stages erected in villages and market places). The play was first read to a group of forty or so peasants in Tolstoy's front room by a good friend, and actor, Stakhovich. The peasants' reactions were not what Tolstoy had expected. Andrey, a young peasant who ran the buffet at Tula station, kept laughing. Tolstoy blamed the reader and not the play, for Andrey's reaction, and he blamed Andrey's laughter for distracting all the other peasants.

Tolstoy to Stakhovich:
"It was all Andrey's fault! Until now he used to look up to you as a sort of general . . . when you tipped him three roubles in the station buffet . . . And all of a sudden you begin to shout, and imitate a

drunkard. How could he help laughing? And his laughing prevented the others from understanding the meaning of the play."

Tolstoy asked an elderly peasant, one of his ex-pupils, what he had made of the play. "What can I tell you Lev Nicholayevich? At first Nikita managed his affairs cleverly, but in the end he proved to be a fool!" Proved to be a fool, by repenting? Tolstoy was deeply upset by this reaction.

A year later the play was read to a very different audience, in the Petersburg Palace of Count Vorontov, in the presence of Tsar Alexander III, the Empress and various dukes and duchesses. Here, it was acknowledged as a work of art. The Tsar wanted to see it on stage and wanted to ensure its success by having a joint company from both the Moscow and St Petersburg Imperial Theatres to act it.

The minister of the Holy Synod, however, Pobyedonostsev, wrote to Alexander III to say that he was so upset when he read the play that he was unable to recover his spirits. He had found the play deeply offensive. "To my knowledge there is nothing like it in any literature. Even Zola never reaches this level of vulgar and brutal realism. . . It is a catastrophe, that as I write to you, enormous numbers of copies of this play have been printed and sold for ten kopecks in cheap booklet form by pedlars on every street corner."

Alexander was alarmed by the minister's letter. He recanted. He wrote to the minister, that although he had much admired the play, he had been 'disgusted' by it. "In my opinion," he wrote, "the play cannot be performed because it is too realistic and its subject matter too horrible." He then went on to write to the Minister of the Interior, "This ignominious Lev Tolstoy must be stopped. He is nothing but a nihilist and a non-believer. It would be advisable to prohibit publication of the play in book form, as the author has already sold enough cheap copies to the people."

The production being rehearsed by the Alexander Theatre in Petersburg was cancelled the night before it was due to open. Shortly afterwards, the censor prohibited the sale of the play in printed form. Faithful to his principles, Tolstoy had already announced through the newspapers that anyone might reproduce copies of his text without having to pay him any royalties. The play was first produced in France by the Théâtre Antoine, in 1888. It was not produced in

Russia until 1895, when Tolstoy was required to rewrite the ending
of Act Four in order to satisfy the censor.

The characters, the brutal reality of the setting, the subject matter and
the story of Tolstoy's play are as alive today as they were when he
wrote it. It would be foolish, however, to pretend, in the act of
translation, that Tolstoy wrote his play in the English of 1980. There
is no British equivalent peasant community, and more than a hundred
years have passed. What I have tried to do, is to capture the energy,
the enthusiasm and the relish that Tolstoy has for peasant dialogue.
Although I have not written the play in any dialect I believe the
brutality and the degradation of the characters' lives is captured in the
imagery of their language. So I have translated most of the idiomatic
phrases literally.

On occasions I have extended or simplified the original in an attempt
to realise its dramatic potential. Only to this extent have I adapted the
piece. The translation is meant to be acted.

This translation was commissioned by Sam Walters, artistic director
of The Orange Tree Theatre. I am extremely grateful for the
encouragement Sam has given me as a writer and director, and for
two years' work in one of London's leading fringe venues. Sam
Walter's remarkable skill as a director was exemplified in his superb
production of this play in 1984. A brilliant cast gave utterly
convincing performances. I would like to thank them all.

                                                    ANTHONY CLARK

THE POWER OF DARKNESS was first performed in this translation at the Orange Tree Theatre, Richmond in 1984. The cast was as follows:

PIOTR IGNATYCH	Peter Wyatt
ANISYA	Roberta Taylor
AKULINA	Madeline Church
ANYUTKA	Annabelle Lanyon
NIKITA	Garry Cooper
MATRIONA	Eve Shickle
AKIM	Geoffrey Leesley
MARINA	Suzie Cerys
MAVRA	Isobil Nisbet
MARTHA	Suzie Cerys
MITRICH	Andrew MacLachlan
IVAN } MARINA'S HUSBAND	Peter Wyatt

DIRECTOR	Sam Walters
SET AND COSTUMES	Caroline Dallas and Ian Sinclair

8

CHARACTERS

PIOTR IGNATYCH   (A rich peasant. 42. Married for a second time. In poor health.)

ANISYA   (His second wife. 32. A smart dresser.)

AKULINA   (Piotr's daughter by his first marriage. 16. Hard of hearing. Simple.)

ANYUTKA   (Piotr's daughter by his second marriage. 10.)

NIKITA   (A labourer. 25. A smart dresser.)

AKIM   (Nikita's father. 50. A pious peasant. Unattractive to look at.)

MATRIONA   (His wife. 50.)

MARINA   (An orphan. 22.)

MITRICH   (An old farm labourer. A retired soldier.)

MARTHA   (Piotr's sister.)

MAVRA   (Anisya's friend.)

NEIGHBOUR   (A woman)

IVAN   (Bridegroom's father. A morose peasant.)

AKULINA'S BRIDEGROOM

MATCHMAKER

BEST MAN

POLICEMAN

COACHMAN

VILLAGE ELDER

GIRL ONE

GIRL TWO

MARINA'S HUSBAND

GUESTS AT THE WEDDING. MEN, WOMEN AND YOUNG CHILDREN.

ACT ONE

Autumn. The action is set in a large peasant village. The scene represents Piotr's spacious cottage. Piotr is sitting on a bench mending a horse's collar. Anisya and Akulina are spinning. The women are singing in two-part harmony.

PIOTR: *(Looking out of the window.)* Those horses have got out again. You see if they don't kill that colt. Nikita! Nikita! Must be deaf.
(Listens to the women.) Be quiet! I can't hear.

NIKITA: *(From the yard.)* What is it?

PIOTR: Fetch in the horses!

NIKITA: That's what I'm doing. All in good time.

PIOTR: *(Shakes his head.)* These farm labourers, they're nothing but trouble. If I were well, I wouldn't bother with them. *(Gets up.)* Nikita! *(Sits down.)* He can't hear me. One of you will have to go. Akulina, fetch them in.

AKULINA: What? The horses?

PIOTR: What d'you think I said?

AKULINA: I'm going.

    Exit.

PIOTR: That lad's a waste of money. He's got the wrong attitude. He's bone idle.

ANISYA: Look who's talking. When you're not flat out on the stove, you're sat on that bench. All you do is boss us about.

PIOTR: If I didn't tell you what to do, within a year there'd be nothing left of this place. You people, you don't know what's good for you.

ANISYA: You expect us to do ten jobs at once. And spend the whole time criticizing us. It's easy to sit there giving orders.

PIOTR: *(Sighs)* If I wasn't so ill, I wouldn't keep him another day.

                Off. Akulina's voice: "Get in! Go on, in there! Shoo. Shoo. In you go." The sound of a colt neighing; horses running through the gate, and the gate crashing shut.

                He's only good at one thing, and that's feeling pleased with himself. He's forever boasting. Honestly, I'd like to sack him.

ANISYA: *(Mimicks Piotr.)* "I'd like to sack him." Let's see you do the work, then you can talk.

AKULINA: *(Enters)* I thought they'd never go in. The roan –

PIOTR: Where's Nikita?

AKULINA: Nikita? In the street.

PIOTR: What's he doing?

AKULINA: What's he doing? He's at the corner talking to someone.

PIOTR: I can't get any sense out of her. Yes, yes, but who's he talking to?

AKULINA: *(Can't hear.)* What?

                Piotr waves Akulina aside. She returns to her spinning.

ANYUTKA: *(Rushes in. To Anisya.)* Nikita's mother and father are here. They want to take him home. I promise you.

ANISYA: You're lying.

ANYUTKA: It's true. I'll die if it isn't! *(Laughing)* I was just walking past, and Nikita says to me, "Goodbye Anna Petrovna," he says. He says, "I'm leaving." And then he burst out laughing.

ANISYA: *(To Piotr.)* That's how much he needs you. He's leaving of his own accord. "I'll sack him," he says.

PIOTR: Let him go. There are plenty more where he came from.

ANISYA: What about the money he's had in advance?

                Anyutka goes to stand in the doorway. She listens to Anisya and Piotr for a while, and then goes out.

PIOTR: *(Frowns)* If it comes to it, he can pay it back, by working for me next summer.

ANISYA: Yes, you're only too pleased to see the back of him. To you, it's one less mouth to feed. All winter I'll have to work like a horse. All on my own. That daughter of yours couldn't care less. And you, you'll be lying on that stove, I know you –

PIOTR: Calm down. Let's find out what's going on.

ANISYA: The farm is full of cattle. You haven't sold the cow. The sheep are all in for the winter. You'll never feed and water them, and you let the labourer go! I won't do a man's work. I'll lie on the stove like you. Let everything go to pot! You do what you like.

PIOTR: *(To Akulina.)* Feeding time. Go and feed the animals.

AKULINA: Is it time to feed the animals? I'll go.

             She puts on her coat, and picks up some rope to tie a bale of straw.

ANISYA: I won't work for you. I've had enough. You can work for yourself.

PIOTR: Ah, stop it! What are you raving about? You're like a sheep with the staggers.

ANISYA: Dog! You don't work. You're a miserable sod. You nag us. You're a rabid dog that won't stop yapping, that's what you are.

PIOTR: *(Spits and puts on his coat.)* Pah! Lord have mercy! Let me find out what's going on.

             Exit.

ANISYA: You decrepit, rat-faced old devil!

AKULINA: Why do you insult Papa?

ANISYA: What's it got to do with you? You idiot. You keep out of this.

AKULINA: *(Heading for the door.)* I know why you insult him. You're the idiot. You stupid bitch. I'm not afraid of you.

ANISYA: What did you say? *(Jumps up, looking for something to strike Akulina.)* If you don't watch it, I'll hit you with that poker.

AKULINA: *(Opening the door.)* You're a bitch! You're the devil! That's what you are, the devil! *(Runs out.)* Devil! Bitch! Devil! Bitch!

ANISYA: *(Reflects)* "Come and enjoy yourself at my wedding. . ." So that's what they have in mind. They intend to marry him off? Nikita, if this is your idea, you wait and see what I'll do. I can't let him go. I can't live without him.

NIKITA: *(Enters. Looks around. Realises that Anisya is on her own. Rushes to her. Whispers.)* Sweetheart, I'm in trouble. My father's come to take me away. He insists I leave. He says I'm to get married, once and for all . . . that I must live at home. I couldn't argue with him.

ANISYA: Well go. See if I care.

NIKITA: What? I wanted to know what to do for the best. "Go." Do you mean that? *(Winks)*

ANISYA: Go ahead, get married! See if I care.

NIKITA: What's wrong with you? You won't even let me touch you. What's the matter?

ANISYA: Nothing. Look, if you want to go, to leave me, well, I don't need you any more. There, I've said it.

NIKITA: Look, stop this. Anisya, I could never forget you, for as long as I live. I'm not going for good. I'll be back. The way I see it, they can marry me off, and as long as I'm not forced to stay at home, I'll be straight back.

ANISYA: And what good will you be to me, married?

NIKITA: Sweetheart, I have to do what my father says.

ANISYA: That's right, blame it on your father. I know who's behind this. I know, you've been planning it for months, with that slut of yours, Marina. She's put you up to it. You see, I know why she was here the other day.

NIKITA: Marina? What do I care about her? There are plenty of
           her type around.

ANISYA: Then why's your father here? You told him to come!
           You've deceived me! *(Cries)*

NIKITA: Anisya, if you believe in God, believe me. I wouldn't
           dream of deceiving you. I know nothing about all this.
           It's got nothing to do with me. It's all in the old man's
           head. His plan.

ANISYA: If you don't want to get married, he can't force you.
           You're not his donkey. You're not a child any more.

NIKITA: But you know what it's like. He's my father. I may not
           want to, but I have to obey him.

ANISYA: All you have to do, is say no, and stick to it.

NIKITA: There was this man who said no. He ended up in the
           district jail where they flogged him until he said "yes".
           I don't want to be beaten. They say it tickles.

ANISYA: Not funny. Listen to me Nikita, if you marry Marina, I
           don't know what I'll do . . . I'll kill myself. I've sinned.
           I've broken the law, but it's too late. There's no going
           back. If you leave me, I'll kill myself. . . .

NIKITA: Leave? Me? If I wanted to leave, I'd have left long
           ago. The other day, Ivan Semenich offered me a job as
           a coachman . . . Would have been an easy life. I know
           I'm good enough to do any job. But I didn't take it. If
           you didn't love me, perhaps I would have done.

ANISYA: Any day, my husband will die. Then, we can hide our
           sin forever. We can get married. You'll be master of
           this farm.

NIKITA: There's no point making plans for the future. I'm not
           bothered. I work as hard for your husband as I would
           for myself. He likes me. And his wife loves me. If
           women will insist on falling in love with me – it's not
           my fault. There's nothing I can do to stop them.

ANISYA: But will you love me forever?

NIKITA: *(Embraces her.)* This much! There'll always be a place
           for you in my heart.

*Matriona enters. She crosses herself in front of the
icons a number of times. Nikita and Anisya separate.*

MATRIONA: What I saw, I didn't see. What I heard, I didn't hear.
Just a bit of fun, eh? Well, a calf will play, so why shouldn't
you? You're still young. Son, the master wants you in the
courtyard.

NIKITA: I was just looking for an axe.

MATRIONA: I know, I know what you were looking for.

NIKITA: *(Bending down to pick up an axe.)* Mama, is it true you
want me to get married? Do I have to? I don't want to.

MATRIONA: My darling, you don't have to do anything you don't
want to. Live life to the full. It's just another one of
your father's crackpot ideas. Run along! We'll sort it
out.

NIKITA: How strange. One minute I have to get married, and
the next I don't. I don't understand what's going on.
Exit.

ANISYA: Aunty Matriona, tell me what's going on? What's
happening? Do you really want him to marry?

MATRIONA: Dear friend, why should we? You know our humble
circumstances. It's the old man talking nonsense. "Get
married. . . He must get married," he says. He's off his
head. Everyone knows you can't budge a horse from a
meal of oats. A man's not going to give up what's good
for him. *(Winks)* Don't think I don't know what's going
on.

ANISYA: There's little escapes you. There's no use hiding it,
Matriona. I've sinned. I'm in love with your son.

MATRIONA: Well, well! You don't say! And Aunty Matriona didn't
know! My dear girl, Aunty Matriona's seen it all
before. She knows what no one knows. My dear, I
know all there is to know. I know young wives find
sleeping powders very useful. Which is why I've
brought you some. *(She unties a knot in her handkerchief
to reveal little paper packets of powder.)* I see what I see.
What I don't see, I don't need to know about. That's
how it is. Matriona was young once. She's had to learn

how to cope, living with her own old fool. I know every
trick in the book. My dear, I can see your old man's on
his last legs. All shrivelled up. It's no life for you. He
wouldn't bleed if you stuck a pitchfork in him. I'm
telling you now, you can bury him in the spring. And
then, you'll need someone else to run this place. Which
brings me back to my son. . . Well? What do you
think? He's as good a choice as any. As far as I'm
concerned there's nothing to be gained by taking him
away from a place where he's needed. Could I be an
enemy to my own flesh and blood?

ANISYA: If only he didn't have to go.

MATRIONA: He's not going anywhere, my dear. I've never heard
             such nonsense. The old man's going senile. He gets an
             idea in his head – ugh, you couldn't knock it out with a
             hammer.

ANISYA: But why?

MATRIONA: Well, my dear. . . you see, Nikita. . . Look, you know
             as well as I do that women find him attractive. He is
             handsome, though I say it myself. Well, when he was
             working on the railway. . . Well, there was this
             orphan. . . A young girl there, who used to cook for
             them. Well, she pursued him –

ANISYA: Marina?

MATRIONA: The devil take her! Whether anything actually
             happened – The old man heard something. Whether it
             was idle gossip, or the girl herself said something to
             him, I don't know.

ANISYA: Cunning bitch!

MATRIONA: Anyway, my idiot husband gets all worked up. "We
             must get him married. . . Married to hide the sin," he
             says. "We must get him home," he witters, "get him
             home . . . get him married. . . ." I argued with him till
             I was blue in the face. Finally I thought I'd try a
             different tack. You have to know how to deal with
             these fools. Pretend to go along with them, but when it
             comes to the crunch, twist everything to suit yourself.
             A woman can think seventy thoughts climbing off the

stove. He never knows what I'm thinking. "Dearest husband," says I, "I agree with you. But we must give the matter more thought. I tell you what, let's go and see Nikita. Let's see what Piotr Ignatych has to say about it." So here we are.

ANISYA: Oh Aunty, I hope it'll be all right. What if his father orders him to marry her?

MATRIONA: Orders? He can stick his orders up a dog's arse. Don't worry, that won't happen. Now, I'd better go and talk to your husband. Not that there's anything to discuss. I only suggested coming to humour the old man. My son is happy, and can expect greater happiness. And I'm supposed to see him marry that slut! D'you think I'm a fool?

ANISYA: But she keeps coming to see him, Marina does. Believe me, aunty, when I heard he was going to get married. . . It felt as if someone had run a knife through my heart. You see, I imagined he loved her.

MARIONA: My dear, the boy's no fool. How could he love some homeless whore? Our Nikita's got more sense. He knows who to love. Now don't worry, we're not going to take him away. He's not going to get married. And if you could give us some money, to tide us over a difficult patch, well, there's no doubt about it, he stays.

ANISYA: If Nikita left me, I think I'd die.

MATRIONA: You're so young. If only you could enjoy life. . . You're a woman in her prime, living with an old fossil.

ANISYA: Believe me, aunty, I'm fed up. Fed up, with the rat-faced old scarecrow. I can't even bear to look at him.

MATRIONA: I know what you're feeling. But – (*Keeping a look out, whispers.*) You know I've been to the old boy that sells the powders. . . He sold me two different sorts. Look. "This one," he says, "is very effective. Give him one dose, and he'll sleep so soundly, you could walk on him and he'd never wake up. But this one here," he says, "is better taken with a drink. There's no smell to it. But it's very strong," he says, "seven doses of this one, a pinch at a time . . . and she'll soon be rid of him."

ANISYA: O-oh! You're not suggesting –

MATRIONA: He says, "It leaves no trace." He wanted a rouble for
            it. "Can't sell it any cheaper," he says. "It's hard to get
            the stuff." I said I'd pay him. You see, I felt sure it
            would be of some use. If not here, then I know old
            Mikhail's daughter –

ANISYA: O-oh! But wouldn't it be wrong –

MATRIONA: Wrong? My dear, if your husband was strong and
            healthy, then it would be a different matter. As it is,
            it's a miracle he's still alive. He's not in the land of the
            living. There are many like him.

ANISYA: Oh, my head! Aunty, I'm scared some evil will come of
            this. No, I couldn't do it.

MATRIONA: All right, I'll have them back.

ANISYA: Do they dissolve in water like other powders?

MATRIONA: Better in tea. "You won't notice anything," he says.
            "No smell, no taste, no nothing." He's a very clever
            man.

ANISYA: *(Taking the powders.)* Oh, my poor head. I'd never do
            this, if my life wasn't such hell.

MATRIONA: You won't forget the rouble? I said I'd pay him as soon
            as possible. You see, he has troubles of his own.

ANISYA: Of course, yes, of course.

            Hides the powders in a chest.

MATRIONA: You won't say a word to anyone about this, will you?
            Don't let anybody know. And if, God forbid, he should
            discover the powders, tell him they're for the
            cockroaches. . . *(She takes the rouble.)* These powders
            are also used to poison cockroaches. It's true.

            Akim enters and crosses himself in front of the icon.

PIOTR: *(Enters and sits down.)* Well, Akim, dear fellow! How
            are things?

AKIM: Better than they were Ignatych. . . Let's say better than
            they were. . . A bit better. It's not right, is it? To
            misbehave, I mean. To play the fool. I want the lad to

get some secure work. And if you would agree to it. . .
Well, it'd be better. . . I think . . . if, well . . .

PIOTR: All right, all right! Sit down, sit down. Tell me what
the problem is.

(Akim sits.)

Well? So you want Nikita to get married?

MATRIONA: We're in no hurry Piotr Ignatych. You know our
humble circumstances. If he were to get married, we
couldn't support ourselves. We can't afford to do
without him.

PIOTR: Well, you must decide what to do for the best.

MATRIONA: I mean, there's no need to rush into marriage, is there?
Marriage can wait. It isn't a raspberry that'll drop off
the bush, if you don't pick it in time.

PIOTR: Perhaps it'd be a good thing for him to get married. . .

AKIM: We would like him to. I would. . . You see, to me. . .
Put it this way, I've found some work in town. . . And
it'll pay well, and. . . It's a good job. . .

MATRIONA: A good job? Emptying cesspools! The other day, he
came back – Ugh! I was sick. Sick as a dog.

AKIM: That's true. At first. . . It knocks you out. The smell, I
mean. . . The smell knocks you out. But then you get
used to it. I mean, it's no worse than the smell of
brewer's malt. The stench. . . Well? What can I say?
We can't afford to find it offensive. . . Us workers. And
then we can always change our clothes. I want. . . I
want Nikita home. He can look after the home, while I
make the money in town.

PIOTR: Yes, I quite understand. You would prefer to have him
at home. But what about the money he's had in
advance?

AKIM: That's true. Very true, Ignatych. . . What you've just
said. . . You've got a point. . . That's right. He put
himself on the market and he managed to get a job.
The contract stands. But. . . But, we must get him

married. He must marry. If you could spare him . . .
spare him, just as long as it takes to. . . Well –

PIOTR: Of course I can.

MATRIONA: We don't agree about this. Piotr Ignatych, let me put it
                to you, as I'd put it to God. Judge between us. My
                husband harps on about how the boy should get
                married. "Get married. He must marry. We must get
                him married. . ." But do you know who he expects
                Nikita to marry? You see, if she was a decent sort, well
                then, I wouldn't stand in his way. I want the best for
                everyone. But the one he has in mind is a degenerate.

AKIM: No. That's not true. You're wrong to insult her like
                that. I mean. . . Because she's . . . the girl. . . My son
                offended. Yes, he offended the girl.

PIOTR: In what way?

AKIM: She got herself involved with him. . . My son. . .
                Involved with Nikita. Nikita, you see. . .

MATRIONA: Don't bother. It'll be easier if I explain. I'll do the
                talking. You know that before coming to work for you,
                our Nikita was working on the railway. And there was
                this girl down there, who cooked for them. . . Well, she
                wouldn't leave him alone. A stupid flirt called Marina.
                Now, she's making all sorts of accusations against our
                son. She claims Nikita deceived her.

PIOTR: Well, that's terrible.

MATRIONA: She's not to be trusted. She's had them all. She's
                nothing but a whore.

AKIM: There you go insulting her again. It's not true. It's
                just. . . Well, it's not all. . . All. . . How shall I put it?
                It's not all –

MATRIONA: (*Mimicks him.*) "How shall I put it. . ." That's all the
                sense you'll get out of the old crock. "How shall I put
                it. . ." He doesn't know what he wants to say. Piotr
                Ignatych, you don't have to listen to me, ask anyone!
                They'll tell you she's a tramp. Good for nothing!

PIOTR: (*To Akim.*) Well, Uncle Akim, if that's the case, there
                seems little point in him marrying her. You can't get

rid of a daughter-in-law, the way you throw out an old
shoe.

AKIM: *(Getting excited.)* It's not true. It's not true. You know
            as well as I do, it's not true! What you say about
            her. . . It's not true. . . Well. . . The girl is good. . . is
            respectable. . . is good. I'm sorry for her. . . The girl, I
            mean. . . I feel sorry for –

MATRIONA: Just like old Miriam, you'll waste tears on the world
            while your family starve. You feel such sympathy for
            the girl, but nothing for your son. If you're really so
            sorry for her, tie her around your neck, and drag her
            with you the rest of your life. I've never heard so much
            nonsense.

AKIM: It's not nonsense.

MATRIONA: Don't interrupt me, I haven't finished!

AKIM: *(Continues)* I know what I'm talking about. You know,
            you twist, you twist everything to suit yourself. . . Even
            when it's got nothing to do with you. . . You must get
            your own way in everything. But God will get his
            way. . . He will.

MATRIONA: I'll shred my tongue talking to you.

AKIM: The girl works hard. . . She's perfectly respectable. . .
            And, well . . . she knows how to look after herself. Poor
            as we are. . . Well. . . It's an extra pair of hands. The
            wedding won't cost much. The most important thing is
            that . . . that. . . . You know, the wrong she's
            suffered. . . She's an orphan and she's been done
            wrong.

MATRIONA: That's what they all say.

ANISYA: Uncle Akim, we're women, we should know. We could
            tell you a thing or two –

AKIM: But God. . . God, I'm telling you. . . That girl is a
            human being. Human. . . And God cares for her. . .
            Think about it.

MATRIONA: He's away.

PIOTR: Uncle Akim, we can't trust these women. Look,

Nikita's here somewhere. Let's get him in, and demand
the truth. He won't want to lose his soul. Go fetch
Nikita. Tell him his father wants to speak to him.

Exit Anisya.

MATRIONA: Let's hear what he has to say for himself, and settle
this once and for all. Nowadays we can't force him to
get married. He must have a say. He'll never consent to
marry her. He wouldn't demean himself. As far as I'm
concerned, he should stay here, and continue to work
for you. He can even work the summer. If we need help
with the harvest, we'll hire someone. Give us ten
roubles, and he can stay.

PIOTR: First things first. Let's settle this before we move on to
anything else.

AKIM: You understand me, don't you Piotr Ignatych. . . You
understand what I'm saying. . . Because, well, these
things happen. . . And we are so concerned to improve
our lot, that we forget about God. . . You know how it
is. . . Just when you think you're doing the right thing,
you're tightening the noose around your neck. You
see. . . If you forget . . . forget about God. The things
you hope will turn out for the best, turn out for the
worst.

PIOTR: Of course. God's will be done at all times.

AKIM: Turn out for the worst. . . But if you're law abiding
and act according to the will of God, you'll be happy in
all that you do. It's the only way to live. So, I think we
must take him home with us . . . the lad, I mean . . . to
marry her. And keep him from the path of sin. He
should stay at home while I earn the money in town.
I'll go out and work. The job's pleasant enough. I
mean, I'm happy. As long as we act according to the
will of God, everything will be all right. You see, she's
an orphan . . . alone in this world . . . and . . . well . . .
like. . . Last summer some men stole wood from the
carpenter's shop. They thought they had got away with
it. They had cheated the carpenter, but not God. So as
long as we act according to God's –

Enter Nikita and Anyutka.

NIKITA: Did someone want to see me?

               Sits down and takes out his tobacco.

PIOTR: (*Quietly, reproachfully.*) Is that the way you behave?
               Your father wants to speak to you – You breeze in,
               plonk yourself down and start rolling your tobacco.
               Stand up! Come here!

               *Nikita gets up and stands by the table. He leans on it,
               casually. He grins.*

AKIM: Well, there's been a complaint made . . . about you.
               Somebody's complained about you. You, Nikita . . .

NIKITA: Who's complained?

AKIM: Who's complained? Well . . . the girl has. The orphan
               girl. . . She has complained, you know. Marina the
               orphan girl has complained about you.

NIKITA: Really? (*Smiles*) What about me? She spoke to you, I
               take it?

AKIM: Now I want to ask you some questions. Now you must
               answer them truthfully. You must tell the truth. Well
               . . . Did you get mixed up with her? I mean, did you
               get yourself involved with her?

NIKITA: I don't know what you're talking about.

AKIM: Playing the fool. . . I mean foolish. Did you do
               anything foolish?

NIKITA: Foolish? Well, it depends what you mean. Yes. When
               we were bored we had to make do with each other for
               entertainment. I used to play the concertina while she
               danced. We were pretty foolish.

PIOTR: Nikita, don't evade the question. You know what your
               father means. Give him a straight answer.

AKIM: (*Solemnly*) Nikita! You can hide from men, but not
               from God. Think before you speak. Don't lie to me.
               She is an orphan. . . A poor orphan. It is so easy to
               take advantage of her. Tell us what really happened.

NIKITA: I've nothing to say. I would tell you the whole story,
               but there's nothing to tell. (*Getting excited.*) She's the

sort of girl who'd say anything! Well let her! Let her say what she wants, as if I were dead and it didn't matter! She had a lot to say about Fedka Mikishin, didn't she? It's impossible to have a bit of honest fun! She can say what she likes.

AKIM: Nikita! A lie will out. Did anything happen?

NIKITA: *(Aside)* He means it.
          (To Akim.) Nothing happened. I've told you all there is to tell. *(Angry)* I swear to God. If I'm lying, let me die now, right here! *(Crosses himself.)* I don't know what you're talking about. *(Silence. Then Nikita continues, his anger increasing.)* So, you've decided I should marry her? It's outrageous! You can't force me to get married. Not any more. Believe me. I swear to you. I know nothing about any of this.

MATRIONA: *(To Akim.)* There! You silly old fool. You let the girl spout you any amount of rubbish, and you swallow it whole. You've hauled him over the coals for nothing. I think he'd better stay here with his master. Piotr Ignatych will give us ten roubles to help out. When the time is right, and only then, will we see our Nikita married.

PIOTR: Well, Uncle Akim, so be it.

AKIM: *(Clicks his tongue.)* You'd better take care, Nikita. The tears of the innocent rain on the guilty. Watch out!

NIKITA: What for? You take care

          Sits.

ANYUTKA: I'll go and tell Mama.

          Rushes out.

MATRIONA: *(To Piotr.)* Well, there you have it Piotr Ignatych, my old man's nothing but trouble to me. He's so stubborn. I'm sorry to have caused you so much inconvenience. Let Nikita stay. Keep him. He's your farm-hand.

PIOTR: Akim?

AKIM: Well . . . I can't force the boy to come home. It's up to him. You see. . . I just wanted –

MATRIONA: You don't know anything about anything. Let him continue living the way he has been living. Let him stay here. He wants to stay. We don't need him at home. We can manage perfectly well without him.

PIOTR: There's just one thing Uncle Akim. If you're going to need him in the summer you may as well take him now. He's not much use during the winter. If he's to stay, it must be for a year.

MATRIONA: Of course, of course for the whole year. He agrees. If we need help with the harvest, we'll hire someone. The boy stays. Now, if you could let us have the ten roubles –

PIOTR: For another year then?

AKIM: (*Sighs*) I suppose so. . . Yes, I suppose so.

MATRIONA: For a year. Starting this Saturday, the feast of St Dimitri. His wages can stay the same, but if you'd be so good as to let us have ten roubles to tide us over, I'd be most obliged.

Rises and bows.

Anisya and Anyutka enter. They sit to one side.

PIOTR: Well? If that's settled then – then let's adjourn to the tavern and wet the bargain. Come on, Uncle Akim, some vodka would do you good.

AKIM: I don't drink . . . drink spirits, I mean.

PIOTR: Tea then?

AKIM: Yes I like my tea. Let's have some tea.

PIOTR: Come on. The women will join us. Nikita, herd the sheep, and rake the straw.

NIKITA: All right.

All leave apart from Nikita. It's getting dark. Nikita lights a cigarette.

They went on and on. They were determined
to find out what I'd been up to. The stories
I could tell. He says I must marry her. If I married
them all, I'd have a lot of wives. Why should I bother
with marriage? I'm as good as married now. All the

advantages, with none of the disadvantages. People
envy me. I don't know what it was that made me cross
myself in front of the icon. That shut them up. They
say you can't swear to something that isn't true.
Rubbish! That you shouldn't. There's nothing to be
scared of. It's easy.

*Akulina enters with the rope. She puts it down, takes off
her coat and goes into the storeroom.*

AKULINA: The least you could do is light the lamp.

NIKITA: To look at you? I can see enough as it is.

AKULINA: Go to hell.

Anyutka runs in.

ANYUTKA: (*Whispers to Nikita.*) Come quick! There's someone to
see you. I promise you there is.

NIKITA: Who is it?

ANYUTKA: Marina. From the railway. She's outside. On the
corner.

NIKITA: You're lying.

ANYUTKA: It's true.

NIKITA: What does she want?

ANYUTKA: She just wants to speak to you. "I must speak to him,"
she said. I asked her what about, and she wouldn't tell
me. She asked me whether it was true you were leaving
us. And I said it wasn't. I told her that your father
wanted to take you away, but that you refused, and that
you were going to stay with us for at least another year.
And then she says, "For God's sake, fetch him for me,
I must speak to him." She's been waiting for ages. You
must go!

NIKITA: To hell with her. Why should I?

ANYUTKA: If you don't go, she'll come and find you. Honest. She
says, "I'll come and find him myself."

NIKITA: She wouldn't dare. She'll wait a bit longer, and then
she'll go.

ANYUTKA: She asked me, "Do they want to marry him to
              Akulina?"

AKULINA: (*Leaving her spinning.*) Marry whom to Akulina?

ANYUTKA: Nikita!

AKULINA: Really? Who says?

NIKITA: That's what they say. (*Looks at her and laughs.*) Akulina,
              will you marry me?

AKULINA: You? If you'd asked me before, I might have said yes.
              But not now.

NIKITA: Not now?

AKULINA: No. Because you won't love me.

NIKITA: Why not?

AKULINA: They won't let you.

NIKITA: Who?

AKULINA: Stepmother, silly! She scolds us, but you can't put a
              foot wrong. She can't keep her eyes off you.

NIKITA: (*Laughs*) You're right. There's nothing that escapes
              you.

AKULINA: I'm not blind, you know. You should have seen her
              today. She exploded at Papa. She was so angry. She
              went for him like a bull, pawing the ground and flaring
              her nostrils. She's a witch!

              Goes into the storeroom.

ANYUTKA: (*Looking out of the window.*) Nikita look! She's coming!
              Nikita, I promise you, she's coming. I'm going.

              Exit.

MARINA: (*Enters*) What are you doing to me?

NIKITA: Doing to you? Nothing.

MARINA: You mean to desert me.

NIKITA: (*Stands up. Angry.*) What did you say?

MARINA: Oh, Nikita!

NIKITA: What the hell are you doing here?

MARINA: Oh, Nikita!

NIKITA: Yes, that's my name. What d'you want? Tell me what you want, or get out!

MARINA: You mean to desert me. To forget.

NIKITA: What? Forget what? There you are, you see, you yourself can't remember. But you came up here, and you sent Anyutka to drag me out. Do you know why I didn't come? I don't need you any more. It's as simple as that. Now, get out!

MARINA: You don't need me any more? I believed you, when you said you loved me. But the minute I'm not around, you don't need me any more.

NIKITA: You're wasting your time. You've tried it on my father. Now go away!

MARINA: But I've never loved anyone else. I don't care whether you marry me or not. It's just that I've never done you any harm, so why have you stopped loving me? Why?

NIKITA: Look, there's no point talking about it. Get out!

MARINA: What really hurts, is not that you've deceived me by promising to marry me, but that you don't love me any more. That you've found someone else! That's what really hurts. And I know who it is.

NIKITA: Why should I waste my time talking to a woman like you? You won't listen to reason. Get out, before I do something stupid.

MARINA: Something stupid? You going to hit me? Come on then! Hit me! You can't bring yourself to, can you? Oh, Nikita!

NIKITA: Someone might come in. And besides what's the point? Look, I've nothing to say to you.

MARINA: So this is it then. The end. Whatever feeling there was between us, has gone. . . You want me to forget everything. Just remember I guarded my maiden's honour, more than my eyes, Nikita. You have ruined me, for nothing. You have deceived me. You take no pity on a poor orphan. *(Cries)* You can deceive me; you can leave me; you can kill me. I bear you no grudge. God forgive you. If you have found somebody better, then you'll soon forget me. But if she's worse, you'll remember. You will, Nikita, I know you will! Goodbye, if I must – But I LOVE YOU! Goodbye forever.

Tries to embrace him, clasping his head in her hands.

NIKITA: *(Tossing back his head.)* What's the point! If you won't go, I will. You stay here!

MARINA: *(Screams)* You bastard! *(In the doorway.)* God never let you be happy!

        Exit, crying.

AKULINA: *(Coming out of the storeroom.)* You're a dog, Nikita!

NIKITA: What's the matter with you?

AKULINA: The way she screamed –

        Cries.

NIKITA: What's it got to do with you?

AKULINA: What? What's it got to do with me? You offended her. And you'll do the same to me. You dog!
        (Going back into the storeroom.)

        Silence.

NIKITA: Chaos. These women – I love them. I've got a sweet tooth for them. Sin with them – Trouble!

        END OF ACT ONE

ACT TWO

The action takes place in the street and in Piotr's cottage. Stage right the cottage in two sections, divided by a passage and porch. Stage left, the yard fence with a gate in it. Six months have passed since Act One. Anisya is stripping hemp near the fence.

ANISYA: *(Stops work.)* He's groaning again. He must've got off the stove.

            Akulina enters carrying a pail on a yoke.

ANISYA: He's calling for something. See what it is he wants. Listen to him!

AKULINA: Why don't you go?

ANISYA: Do as you're told!

            Akulina goes into the cottage.

ANISYA: He's worn me out. He won't tell me where he's put the money, and that's that. The other day, he was in the hall. . . It's got to be in there, somewhere. But where? I suppose I should be grateful he won't part with it. At least I know it's still here. But if only I knew where! I'm sure he had it on him yesterday. Now, I don't know where it is. I'm worn out, body and soul.

            Akulina enters, tying on a head scarf.

ANISYA: Where do you think you're going?

AKULINA: Where am I going? He told me to go to Aunt Martha's. He says, "Tell my sister I need her. I'm dying." He says, "I must talk to her."

ANISYA: *(To herself.)* So he wants to see his sister, does he? Oh dear. O – oh, that means he's going to give it to her. What am I going to do? O! *(To Akulina.)* Don't go! Where d'you think you're going?

AKULINA: To fetch Aunt Martha.

ANISYA: Don't go. I'll go. You do as you're told. Take the washing down to the stream. Get going or you'll still be at it this evening!

AKULINA: But he told me to go.

ANISYA: Do as I say! I'll go and fetch Aunt Martha. Bring the
             shirts in off the fence.

AKULINA: The shirts? I know you, you won't go. He told me to go.

ANISYA: Look, I said I'd go, so I'll go. Where's Anyutka?

AKULINA: Anyutka? Minding the calves.

ANISYA: Fetch her here. They won't stray.

             Akulina picks up the washing and goes out.

ANISYA: If I don't go, he'll scold me. If I go . . . and he gives
             his sister the money, then I'll have been to all this
             trouble for nothing. I don't know what to do. I can't
             think straight.

             Continues to strip hemp.
             Matriona enters wearing heavy outdoor clothes. She's
             walking with a stick. She's carrying a bundle.

MATRIONA: God be with you, my dear. How are you?

ANISYA: *(Throws her arms up in joy.)* You gave me such a start.
             What a surprise. God has sent you, in the nick of time.

MATRIONA: Why, what's the matter? What's happened?

ANISYA: I'm going out of my mind. It's terrible!

MATRIONA: Still alive then?

ANISYA: Only just. I can't tell you how terrible it's been. He
             won't die.

MATRIONA: What about the money?

ANISYA: He's just sent for his sister, Martha. I'm sure he'll give
             it to her –

MATRIONA: You're sure he hasn't given it to anyone else?

ANISYA: Positive. I've been watching him like a hawk.

MATRIONA: Where is it then?

ANISYA: He won't tell me. I don't know. He keeps moving it
             from one hiding place to another. And Akulina's always
             hovering about, which doesn't help. She may be an

idiot, but she's watching me all the time. O-oh! My
poor head! I'm at the end of my tether.

MATRIONA: My dear, if someone else gets that money, you'll weep
the rest of your life. They'll throw you out of this
house, with nothing. You've drudged my precious . . .
drudged for a man you don't love. . . As a widow you'll
walk with a beggar's pouch, if –

ANISYA: Don't! Don't even suggest such a fate! My heart aches.
I don't know what to do. There's nobody to help me. I
told Nikita. He flinched. He wouldn't have anything to
do with it. The only thing he's done – Yesterday he
told me the money was under the floorboards.

MATRIONA: And?

ANISYA: Well, I haven't had a chance to look, because the old
man hasn't left the room. You see, the problem is that
one minute he's got it on him and the next he's hidden
it somewhere.

MATRIONA: Well my dear, if you let the money go, you'll never
forgive yourself. Your life will never be the same.
(Whispers) Did you give him some of that strong tea?

ANISYA: O – oh!

*She is about to reply when she catches sight of her
neighbour.*

Mavra enters. She passes the cottage.

MAVRA: *(To Anisya.)* Anisya! Anisya! Good neighbour! Your
husband's calling for you.

ANISYA: No, no, that's just him coughing. It sounds like he's
calling someone. He's in a terrible state.

MAVRA: *(To Matriona.)* Good day, old woman. Where've you
come from?

MATRIONA: Home dear, where else. I've come to see Nikita. He's
my son. I've brought him some new shirts. One has to
look after one's own.

MAVRA: Certainly one does. *(To Anisya.)* I want to start
bleaching the linen, but I think I'm too early. Nobody
else has started.

ANISYA: There's no hurry.

MATRIONA: Has he had communion?

ANISYA: Yes, the priest was here yesterday.

MAVRA: My dear, yesterday he was barely alive. When I saw
             him. . . I just can't believe how much he's wasted
             away. The other day he was so close to death, they laid
             him out under the icons. They started to keen, and
             were preparing to wash the body –

ANISYA: When he suddenly recovered. He got up and started
             creeping about again.

MATRIONA: Is he going to be given extreme unction?

ANISYA: I've been told it's important. If he's still alive we'll
             send for the priest tomorrow.

MAVRA: It's so hard on you Anisya. But don't they always say,
             the one that does the looking after suffers the most.

ANISYA: You have no idea how difficult it's been.

MAVRA: I can imagine. He's been about to die for nearly a year.
             You've been bound, hand and foot.

MATRIONA: It won't be any easier for you as a widow. Ah, it'll be
             all right while you're young, but when you're old
             nobody could care less. Old age is a misery. Look at
             me, I haven't come far, and I'm exhausted. My feet are
             numb. Where's my son?

ANISYA: He's busy, ploughing the fields. You must come in,
             we'll start the samovar. Tea will revive you.

MATRIONA: I'm so tired, my dears. You know, I think he ought to
             have extreme unction, they say it frees the soul.

ANISYA: Don't worry, I'll get the priest tomorrow.

MATRIONA: Good. You know there's been a wedding in our district.

MAVRA: During Lent?

MATRIONA: Yes, you know what they say, "A poor man marries
             before the night is through." Semyen Matvyeich has
             married Marina.

ANISYA: So she's got herself a husband.

MAVRA: He's a widower, isn't he? That means she's looking
            after the children.

MATRIONA: All four of them. No decent girl would have him. Still,
            he chose her. The wine may have overflowed, but you
            know what they say, never drink out of a cracked glass!

MAVRA: Well how's it going? He's rich isn't he?

MATRIONA: So far so good.

MAVRA: What sort of woman would marry a man with four
            children? There's our Mikhail, my dear. Now there's a
            man desperate to find –

VOICE OFF: Hey Mavra! Where the devil are you? Bring in the cow.

            Mavra leaves.

MATRIONA: Well my dear, that's Marina out of harm's way. My old
            man needn't give her another thought. *(Once Mavra is
            out of the way, whispers.)* She's gone. Where was I? Oh
            yes, did you give him some tea?

ANISYA: Don't talk about it. I'd prefer he died a natural death.
            Besides they don't work. He won't die. And I'm left
            with the sin on my conscience. Oh! My poor head!
            Why did you ever have to give them to me?

MATRIONA: What? The powders? Why shouldn't I sell you sleeping
            powders? There's nothing wrong with them.

ANISYA: Not the sleeping powders. The other powder, the white
            powder in the other packet.

MATRIONA: My dear, they were for medicinal use only.

ANISYA: *(Sighs)* I know. . . I know. . . I'm so afraid. . . He's
            worn me out.

MATRIONA: How much have you given him?

ANISYA: I've given it to him twice.

MATRIONA: Did he suspect anything?

ANISYA: I tasted the powder myself. It's very bitter. He drank it
            down with his tea, and then said, "I'm so sick, this tea
            tastes revolting." I said, "Everything tastes bitter when
            you're ill." Matriona, I was terrified.

MATRIONA: Don't think about it. The more you think about it, the worse you'll feel.

ANISYA: I wish you hadn't given them to me, and led me to sin. You've scorched my soul. Why did you have to give me that powder?

MATRIONA: What d'you mean? Anisya, Christ have mercy on you. Why blame me? You'll see, it'll do you no good accusing the innocent. If something goes wrong. . . I know nothing about it. It's got nothing to do with me. I'll kiss the cross and swear that I never gave you the powder . . . that I never knew such powder existed. No, you'll have to think for yourself. But my dear, I know how difficult it's been for you. Just the other day we were talking about you. "The poor thing. . . She has to suffer so much. Her stepdaughter's a fool. Her husband's nothing but skin and bone. . . ." And someone said, "If I were in her situation, there's nothing I wouldn't do to make life more bearable!"

ANISYA: That's how I feel. I've had enough of this wretched life. I'm ready to hang myself. I could strangle him. This life isn't worth living!

MATRIONA: That's more like it. Now, don't just stand there – Find out where that money is, and make sure he has some more tea.

ANISYA: Poor me. I don't know what to do. I'm so scared. If only he'd die a natural death. I don't want to burden my soul.

MATRIONA: (*Angry*) Why won't he show you where it is? Does he want it buried with him? To leave it to no one? I ask you, is it right? God forbid, that such a large sum of money should go to waste. It'd be a sin! What is he playing at? Let me see him!

ANISYA: I don't know any more. He's worn me out.

MATRIONA: What d'you mean, you don't know? It's as simple as this: if you give up now, you'll never forgive yourself. He'll give the money to his sister, and that'll be the last you see of it.

ANISYA: Oh dear. . . That's right. . . He sent for her. I must go
              and fetch her.

MATRIONA: Not yet. First things first. Light the samovar. We'll
              give him some tea and then we'll both look for the
              money. Don't worry, I'm sure we'll find it.

ANISYA: O – oh! But what if something goes wrong?

MATRIONA: Look, what's the matter with you? You've come this
              far, and now you decide to give up. It's within reach
              and you're prepared to let it go. Come on.

ANISYA: I'll light the samovar.

MATRIONA: That's more like it. You won't regret it.

              Anisya walks away. Matriona calls her back.

MATRIONA: Wait Anisya! There's just one thing – Look, don't tell
              Nikita about any of this. He's still a bit young. If he
              found out about the powder, I don't know what he'd
              do. He's such a sensitive soul. As a young boy, I
              couldn't even get him to strangle a chicken. Don't say
              anything. You see, he just wouldn't understand –
              (She stops, horror-struck.)

              *Piotr appears in the doorway. He clings to the wall as
              he makes his way to the porch. He calls out. His voice
              is weak.*

PIOTR: Didn't you hear me call? O – oh! Anisya, who's there?
              (Falls on to a bench.)

ANISYA: *(Steps from behind a corner.)* What are you doing? You
              shouldn't be out here. You should've stayed where you
              were.

PIOTR: Has Akulina gone to fetch Martha? This pain is
              unbearable. If only I could die quickly . . .

ANISYA: She was too busy. I sent her down to the stream. If
              you'd give us time, I'll go and fetch Martha myself.

PIOTR: Anyutka. . . Send Anyutka. Where is she? Ahh! This
              searing pain. I'm dying . . .

ANISYA: I've sent for her.

PIOTR: Where is she?

ANISYA: I don't know. I don't know why she's not here yet,
           devil take her!

PIOTR: This pain is unbearable. My insides burn. It's as if a
           gimlet were drilling into my gut. Why do you treat me
           like a dog? Why do you leave me on my own? No one
           even bothers to give me a drink. O – oh! Send Anyutka
           to me!

ANISYA: Here she comes. Anyutka, your father wants to speak to
           you.

           Anyutka rushes in. Anisya retires around the corner.

PIOTR: Go. . . o – oh! Go and tell Aunt Martha that your
           father wants to speak to her. To see her. Tell her to
           come here.

ANYUTKA: Is that it?

PIOTR: Wait. Tell her to be quick. Tell her, I'm ready to
           die. . . Ahhh! O – oh!

ANYUTKA: I'll be as quick as I can.

           Runs out.

MATRIONA: (*Winks to Anisya.*) Remember what to do. Go inside.
           Search high and low. Be as thorough as a dog searching
           for fleas. Leave no stone unturned. I'll look after the
           old man.

ANISYA: (*To Matriona.*) All right. I feel stronger when there are
           two of us. (*To Piotr.*) Would you like me to light the
           samovar? Aunty Matriona's here. She's come to see her
           son. I thought we might all have some tea together. . .

PIOTR: Light the samovar. . .

           Anisya goes into the cottage.

MATRIONA: (*To Piotr. She bows.*) Good day to you, Piotr Ignatych.
           Benefactor, dear friend. . . How are you? Still sick. . .
           My husband sympathises. "Go and see Piotr, see how
           he is. . . Poor man, see how he is!" He sends his best
           wishes.

           She bows again.

PIOTR: I'm dying.

MATRIONA: When I look at you, Piotr Ignatych, I realise man
              suffers more pain than any creature on God's earth.
              You've simply wasted away. You're nothing but skin
              and bone. Illness has eroded your good looks.

PIOTR: I'm near to death.

MATRIONA: Piotr Ignatych, you have had communion, and, God
              willing, you'll receive extreme unction. Your wife,
              thanks be to God, is a sensible woman. You'll receive a
              proper burial and prayers will be said for your soul.
              Everything will be done as it should be done. You
              don't need to worry about anything. My son will look
              after the farm as long as is necessary.

PIOTR: There's no one to manage the farm. My wife's too
              neglectful. All she thinks about is having a good time.
              You see, I know. . . I know everything. Akulina's
              simple, and besides she's too young. I started from
              scratch. . . From nothing. I built this place up to what
              it is today. Now there's nobody to take over. Such a
              pity.
              (Snivels)

MATRIONA: Well, if you're worried about the money. . . Perhaps
              you'd like to tell me what you –

PIOTR: *(Catching sight of Anisya.)* Has Anyutka left?

MATRIONA: *(Aside)* He hasn't forgotten.

ANISYA: She's gone. She's collected her hat and scarf, she's
              gone. Come on in. Here, I'll help you.

PIOTR: No, let me sit here . . . for the last time. . . . It's too
              stuffy in there. I feel terrible. My heart burns. If only I
              could die.

MATRIONA: God controls life and death Piotr Ignatych. There's no
              telling what might happen. You might suddenly
              recover. There was this peasant in our village. . . Well,
              he was on his deathbed when –

PIOTR: No. I can feel it. I know I'll die today. I can feel it.

              Leans against the wall and closes his eyes.

ANISYA: *(Enters)* Are you coming? I can't wait here all day.
              Piotr? Piotr?

MATRIONA: *(Beckons Anisya to one side.)* Well?

ANISYA: Nothing.

MATRIONA: Are you sure you looked everywhere? Under the floorboards?

ANISYA: There's nothing there. Perhaps it's in the shed. He was in there yesterday.

MATRIONA: Well, keep looking. Leave no stone unturned. Lick the place clean. I tell you, he'll die today. His nails are blue, and his face as cold as the earth. Is the samovar ready?

ANISYA: It's just about to boil.

            Nikita arrives on the other side of the stage. If possible, on horse back. He doesn't see Piotr.

NIKITA: Hello Mama, how are things at home?

MATRIONA: Thank the Lord, we live while there's bread to eat.

NIKITA: And have you seen the master? How is he?

MATRIONA: Shh! He's resting. Over there.

            Points to the porch.

NIKITA: I don't care if he never gets better. He can stay like that.

PIOTR: *(Opens his eyes.)* Nikita! Nikita! Come here!

            Nikita goes to Piotr, Anisya and Matriona whisper to each other.

PIOTR: Why are you back so early?

NIKITA: I finished.

PIOTR: Did you plough that strip of land beyond the bridge?

NIKITA: It was too far.

PIOTR: Too far? You'll have even further to walk from here. Back you go. You should've done it all the first time.

            Anisya listens to their conversation surreptitiously.

MATRIONA: *(To Nikita.)* Nikita, why don't you try to please him? Your master's so ill. He relies on you. You ought to work as hard for him as you would for your own father. Strain every muscle. Do the job well. Haven't I always said, strain every muscle to do the job well.

PIOTR: O – oh! This terrible pain. Go and dig the potatoes! Ah! The women can sort them.

ANISYA: *(To herself.)* I'm staying here. He's trying to get us all out of the way. He's probably got the money on him, and he wants to hide it somewhere.

PIOTR: Otherwise – Ahhh! . . . when the time comes to plant them, they'll be rotten. I can't stand this pain.

             He gets up.

MATRIONA: *(Rushes to support him.)* Let me help you.

PIOTR: Take me in. Nikita!

NIKITA: *(Angry)* What is it?

PIOTR: This is the last time I'll see you. . . I'll die today. . . You must forgive me. . . Forgive me, in the name of Jesus Christ our Lord. If I've sinned against you, in word and deed. . . Whenever I've sinned against you. . . Many times. . . Please forgive me!

NIKITA: But we're all sinners. So what?

MATRIONA: Nikita, show some feeling for the poor man.

PIOTR: Forgive me, in the name of Christ.
             (Weeps)

NIKITA: *(Breathing heavily.)* God will have mercy on you, Uncle Piotr. I bear you no grudge. You've never treated me badly. You must forgive me! I've treated you far worse than you've treated me. I've sinned against you.
             (Cries)

             Piotr leaves, snivelling, supported by Matriona.

ANISYA: Oh dear. . . My poor head! He's up to something. I know he is. It's obvious. *(To Nikita.)* You said the money was under the floorboards. It's not there.

NIKITA: *(Crying)* He's always been good to me. . . Just think of the terrible things I've done to him. . .

ANISYA: Pull yourself together. Where's the money?

NIKITA: *(Angry)* How should I know? Look for it yourself!

ANISYA: I see, so now you're feeling sorry for him . . .

NIKITA: Yes, I'm feeling sorry for him! Just look at the way he
            started to cry. I feel sorry for him.

ANISYA: You pity him, do you? You're overcome with pity. But
            the man treated you like a dog – A DOG! Just before
            you arrived, he was telling us that he wanted you out!
            To get rid of you. You'd do better feeling sorry for me.

NIKITA: Why should I feel sorry for you?

ANISYA: Well, he's going to die; he'll cut me out of his will;
            hide the money –

NIKITA: Maybe he won't.

ANISYA: But dear Nikita, he's sent for his sister. He'll give it to
            her, all of it. And it'll be our bad luck. How will we
            cope without that money? I'll be forced out of the
            house. You must help me, Nikita. You said he was in
            the shed, yesterday evening, . . Was he?

NIKITA: I just saw him coming out. I don't know where he's
            hidden it!

ANISYA: Oh dear. . . Poor me. I'll go and have a look.

            *Matriona comes out of the cottage, down the steps of the
            porch, to Nikita and Anisya.*

MATRIONA: *(Whispers)* Stay where you are. The money's on him. I
            felt it. It's tied round his neck.

ANISYA: Oh, my poor head.

MATRIONA: Let him out of our sight and it's gone for good. When
            his sister gets here, you can wave it goodbye.

ANISYA: She'll come. He'll give it to her. What can I do? My
            poor head.

MATRIONA: What can you do? I'll tell you what you can do. The
            samovar's boiled, go and make the tea. Pour him a cup.
            (Whispers) Unfold the little paper packet . . . you know
            the one I mean, sprinkle the powder, all of it, into the

cup. When he's finished his tea, untie the string. Don't worry, he won't cry out.

ANISYA: But I'm so afraid.

MATRIONA: There's no time to waste. Get on with it. I'll deal with the sister if she gets here before you're finished. Don't bungle it. Untie the money; bring it here, and Nikita will hide it.

ANISYA: My head's spinning. Where do I start?

MATRIONA: Come on, now, get on with it. Do exactly what I said. Nikita!

NIKITA: What?

MATRIONA: Stay here. Sit on the bench, just in case you're needed.

NIKITA: *(Dismissing her.)* You women, what'll you think of next? I've had enough. I'm going to dig the potatoes.

MATRIONA: *(Catching him by the arm.)* Stay here!

            Enter Anyutka.

ANISYA: Well?

ANYUTKA: She was at her daughter's house. She was in the garden. She's on her way.

ANISYA: What happens when she arrives?

MATRIONA: *(To Anisya.)* Don't you worry about that! Just go and do as I said.

ANISYA: But I don't know what to do. I don't know anything, any more. My mind's so confused. Anyutka, dear child, go and mind the calves. O – oh! I can't –

            Anyutka runs out.

MATRIONA: Go on, get on with it. I should think the water's boiled dry.

ANISYA: Oh my poor head! My poor, poor head!
            Exit.

MATRIONA: *(To Nikita.)* Well, there we are, son . . . *(Sitting beside him on the bench.)* You see, we have to think about your prospects. No good leaving it to chance.

NIKITA: What do you mean, prospects?

MATRIONA: Your future livelihood.

NIKITA: Livelihood? I'll get by, the same as everybody else.

MATRIONA: The old man. . . He'll die today. . .

NIKITA: And go to heaven. What's it got to do with me?

MATRIONA: *(From time to time, glancing in the direction of the porch.)*
            The living must live. We live by our wits. Think how
            much I've done for you. I've run my legs off, the
            trouble I've taken. So you won't forget me in my hour
            of need, will you?

NIKITA: What are you talking about? What've you done? Why
            put yourself to any trouble?

MATRIONA: All for the sake of your future. For your sake. If you
            don't take a little trouble, nothing is achieved. You
            know Ivan Moseich? Well, I went to see him the other
            day. There was something I wanted to get straight. I
            sat there, and we talked. "Ivan Moseich," I says, "tell
            me, what would you do in this instance. . . Let's say,
            there's this peasant widower, and he marries again. . .
            And let's say that he has children. One daughter by his
            first wife, and one daughter by his second. Well," I
            says, "if the old peasant were to die, is it possible for
            another peasant to marry his widow and get the farm?
            And is it possible for this peasant to marry off the
            daughters, and remain master of that farm?" "It's all
            possible," he says, "but you'll have to put yourself to a
            bit of trouble. If the money's right," he says, "it can be
            done. Without the money you can forget the whole
            idea."

NIKITA: *(Laughs)* He was after your money. People are always
            after your money.

MATRIONA: My darling, I explained everything to him. Then he
            says, "First your son must get himself on the village
            register. But he'll need money for this – To buy the
            village elders a drink. They'll do it!" He says to me,
            "Everything must be carefully thought through." Look
            at this! *(Removes a piece of paper from her scarf.)* Read it
            to me.

NIKITA: It's just a legal document. No words of wisdom.

MATRIONA: "Aunty," he says, "it's most important that you don't
               let the money out of your sight. The wife must get the
               money, or she'll never be able to marry off the
               daughters. Money is the key to the whole business," he
               says, "don't let it go!" So we'll see it through, eh?

NIKITA: What's it got to do with me? It's her money. She can
               do what she likes with it.

MATRIONA: Don't be stupid! She's not the sort that can cope on
               her own. If she gets the money, she won't know what
               to do with it. Let's face it, she's a woman and you're a
               man. You'll know what to do for the best. You'll put
               the money away for her. You're more sensible than she
               is. Then if anything were to happen, it'd be safe.

NIKITA: You women don't understand anything.

MATRIONA: What? Look, just get the money, and you'll be in
               charge. When she starts to grumble you can pull in the
               reins.

NIKITA: To hell with all of you. I'm going.

               Anisya runs out of the house, looking very pale.

ANISYA: It was on him. I've got it. Here.

               Points under her apron.

MATRIONA: Give it to Nikita. He'll put it somewhere safe. Nikita,
               take it. Hide it.

NIKITA: Give it to me, then!

ANISYA: I'm so confused. I'll hide it myself.

               Rushes to the gate.

MATRIONA: *(Grabbing Anisya's arm.)* Where do you think you're
               going? His sister's due any minute. She'll find it
               strange, you not being here. Give it to Nikita. He
               knows what to do. How can you be so stupid!

ANISYA: I'm so confused.

NIKITA: Then give it to me. I'll hide it.

ANISYA: Where?

NIKITA: You don't trust me, eh?
            (Laughs)

            Akulina enters with the washing.

ANISYA: O – oh! My poor head. *(Gives the money to Nikita.)* Be
            careful, Nikita!

NIKITA: What's the matter? You afraid I'll forget where I put
            it?

            Exit.

ANISYA: *(Terrified)* Oh dear, but what if he –

MATRIONA: Is he dead?

ANISYA: Yes. He seemed it. He didn't move when I took the
            money.

MATRIONA: You'd better go inside, here comes Akulina.

ANISYA: I'm the one that has sinned, but he's got the money –

MATRIONA: That's enough of that. Inside! Here comes Martha.

ANISYA: I trusted him. What's going to happen?

            Exit.

            Martha and Anyutka enter.

MARTHA: *(To Akulina.)* I know I should have been here sooner.
            It's just that I was at my daughter's and – Well, how is
            he? Dying?

AKULINA: *(Sorting the washing.)* I don't know. I've been down at
            the stream.

MARTHA: *(Pointing to Matriona.)* Who's that? Where does she
            come from?

MATRIONA: From Zuyev. I'm Nikita's mother. I'm from Zuyev, my
            dear. Good day to you! Your dear brother is fading
            fast, fading fast. . . He struggled out here, all on his
            own. "Fetch my sister," he says, "because –" O – oh!
            It's too late!

                *Anisya rushes out of the house, with a terrible cry. She
                clings to the post, that holds up the roof of the porch, and
                starts to wail.*

ANISYA: O – o – oh! Why have you left me? O – o – oh! Why
             have you deserted me? O – o – oh! I'm a poor
             wretched widow. . . His shining eyes are shut tight . . .
             forever and ever . . .

                   *Enter various peasants. Mavra and Matriona support
                   Anisya. Akulina and Martha go inside. A crowd gathers.*

VOICE IN
CROWD: Call the old women to lay out the body!

MATRIONA: *(Rolling up her sleeves.)* Is there any water in the kettle?
             There'll be some in the samovar.

                   END OF ACT TWO

ACT THREE

Piotr's cottage. Nine months later. Anisya, shabbily dressed, sits at the loom, weaving. Anyutka is on the stove.

MITRICH: *(Enters, slowly. Takes off his coat.)* O Lord have mercy! Is the master back?

ANISYA: What?

MITRICH: Nikita? Is he back from town?

ANISYA: Not yet.

MITRICH: He'll be living it up. O Lord!

ANISYA: You finished threshing?

MITRICH: What do you think? I left the place tidy. I covered the floor with straw. I don't like to leave a job half done. O Lord! Blessed St Nicholas! Ach, it's high time he was back.

Picks at his callouses.

ANISYA: Why should he hurry. He's got plenty of money. He'll be up to no good with that girl. . .

MITRICH: Well, if you've got the money, spend it! Enjoy yourself. Why did Akulina go?

ANISYA: Ask her. I don't know.

MITRICH: Why would she have gone? I suppose, when you've got th money, there's a lot to buy. O Lord!

ANYUTKA: Mama, I know why. "I'll buy you a little shawl – ly – wawly," he says. Honest, that's what he said to her. "You can choose it yourself," he says. And so she gets herself all dressed up in her velvet jacket and French shawl –

ANISYA: There you are! A girl keeps her maiden honour to the door. . . When she crosses the threshold she leaves it behind. She's got no shame, that one.

MITRICH: There, there. . . What's she got to be ashamed of? They've got the money, so let them enjoy themselves. O Lord! Is it supper time?

(No answer.)

Well then, I'll go warm myself up. *(Climbs on the stove.)* O Lord . . . Holy Mary, Mother of God . . . Blessed St Nicholas . . . have mercy on us!

NEIGHBOUR: *(Enters)* He's still not back?

ANISYA: No.

NEIGHBOUR: He's very late. Most likely stopped off for a drink. My dear, my sister Thekla says, there're a lot of sledges pulled up outside the tavern. All back from town.

ANISYA: Anyutka, Anyutka!

ANYUTKA: What?

ANISYA: Anyutka, run over to the tavern and see if you can find him. If he's drunk, that's where he'll be.

NEIGHBOUR: Did he take Akulina?

ANISYA: She was his reason for going. She's his "business" in town. "I must go to the bank," he says, "to collect the interest." She's nothing but trouble.

NEIGHBOUR: *(Shaking her head.)* Such goings on!

    Silence.

ANYUTKA: *(In the doorway.)* If he's there, what do I say?

ANISYA: Don't say anything. Just see if he's there.

ANYUTKA: I'll be as quick as I can. *(Runs out.)*

    A long silence.

MITRICH: *(Bellows)* O Lord! Blessed Nicholas!

NEIGHBOUR: *(Starts)* O – oh! That gave me quite a start. Who is it?

ANISYA: Mitrich. Our labourer.

NEIGHBOUR: Dear me, he gave me such a fright. I'd forgotten he was here. Dear friend, they tell me the matchmaker has been to see Akulina. . . .

ANISYA: *(Moving out from behind the loom to sit at the table.)* A family from Dedlovo were interested. But they must have heard something. They expressed an interest, but it went no further than that. Who would want her?

NEIGHBOUR: What about the Lizunovs from Zuyev?

ANISYA: It came to nothing. Nikita wouldn't co-operate.

NEIGHBOUR: She ought to be married by now.

ANISYA: Of course she should. I can't wait to get her out of the house. But my dear, it's easier said than done. He doesn't want her to go. So she won't. He hasn't yet tired of her.

NEIGHBOUR: Ahh! The sin. It doesn't bear thinking about. He's her stepfather.

ANISYA: I was completely taken in. I'm such a fool. I didn't realise it was happening. It didn't even cross my mind. I didn't suspect anything when I married him, but they were already in cahoots.

NEIGHBOUR: What a terrible business.

ANISYA: It went from bad to worse. They hide so much from me. I'm sick of it. My life's a misery. It'd be all right, if I didn't still love him!

NEIGHBOUR: You don't have to tell me.

ANISYA: It hurts. I suffer his behaviour. It hurts.

NEIGHBOUR: They say he raises a hand to you –

ANISYA: That too. He used to be gentle when he was drunk. Playful. Now, when he's had a few too many he lets fly at me. He wants to beat me, to trample me underfoot. The other day he somehow got his hand tangled in my hair. And as I tried to free myself, he pulled and pulled. As for Akulina, she's worse than a snake. I didn't know such poisonous creatures existed.

NEIGHBOUR: Oh dear, dear Anisya, the more I think about it, the more terrible your situation seems to me. How can you bear it? You took the beggar in, and in return he torments you! You should show him what you're made of.

ANISYA: If only I could get you to understand. . . You see, my

heart still yearns for him. My late husband was a
tyrant, but I could get him to do whatever I wanted.
Now it's different. I only have to look at Nikita and my
heart melts. I haven't got the strength to confront him.
I feel like a wet hen. Helpless.

NEIGHBOUR: Dearest neighbour, it's obvious, you're bewitched. That
Matriona woman, they say she's a witch. She's put a
spell on you.

ANISYA: You may be right. There are times when it hurts so. . .
I just want to tear him to pieces. And then when I see
him, I can't . . . my heart won't let me.

NEIGHBOUR: I'm telling you, you're bewitched. Your body's been
poisoned. You'll waste away. Look at you.

ANISYA: I know. I'm as thin as a rake. And that fool Akulina –
You know, there was a time when she was slovenly
and sluttish. A time past. She's changed. He's dressed
her up. She parades her finery. . . She's all puffed up,
like a bubble on water. It doesn't matter that she's
stupid, she's got it into her head that she's now
mistress of the house. "This house is mine," she says.
"Papa always wanted me to marry Nikita." At times
she can be so spiteful. God have mercy on us! When
she loses her temper, she tears straw from the thatch.

NEIGHBOUR: What a life, Anisya! And there are people that envy
you. "They're rich," they say. Gold won't stop tears.

ANISYA: There's nothing to be envious of. The money will
disappear like dust. It's terrible the way he squanders
it.

NEIGHBOUR: Why do you give him so much? It's your money.

ANISYA: If only you knew the whole story. I made one small
mistake.

NEIGHBOUR: In your position. I'd go straight to the law. It's your
money. How dare he squander it? He's no right to.

ANISYA: Rights don't come into it.

NEIGHBOUR: But my dear friend, when I look at you – You're so
weak.

ANISYA: As weak as weak can be. I'm trapped. I don't know
            what to do. I'm in such a state.

NEIGHBOUR: There's somebody coming.

            She listens. The door opens.

AKIM: *(Enters. Crosses himself; shakes the snow off his bast shoes
            and takes off his coat.)* Peace be with you! Peace to all
            those that live in this house! How are you all? *(To
            Anisya.)* Good evening, my dear.

ANISYA: How are you, Father? Did you come straight here?
            Come on, sit yourself down.

AKIM: I thought. . . Well, I'd ask – I mean, I wanted to see
            my son. I've come to see him. I didn't set off too early.
            I mean, I made sure I had something to eat, before
            coming out. But, there's so much snow. . . It's difficult
            to get anywhere. . . It was hard going, I'm telling you.
            I'm later than I expected. Is he in?

ANISYA: No. He went into town. He's not back yet.

AKIM: *(Sits on the bench.)* I've something I want to discuss
            with him. It's a business matter. I told him – You see,
            we're in – Well, the other day I told him there was
            something we needed. I told him, our old horse was on
            her last legs. You know, our dear old horse. . . Worn
            out, exhausted. We must get a new one. I mean we
            can't manage without. That's why I'm here.

ANISYA: Nikita will talk to you when he gets back. *(Goes to the
            stove.)* Have some supper. He'll be back soon. Mitrich!
            Hey Mitrich! Supper time!

MITRICH: What?

ANISYA: Supper.

MITRICH: O Lord, blessed St Nicholas!

ANISYA: Come and eat your supper.

NEIGHBOUR: I'll be off then. Goodbye.

            Exit.

MITRICH: *(Getting off the stove.)* I must've fallen asleep. O Lord,

Blessed St Nicholas! I must've fallen asleep. Good
evening, Uncle Akim.

AKIM: Ah, Mitrich! Why are you? I mean, what are you doing
here?

MITRICH: I'm working for your son. I live here.

AKIM: What? Working for my son? Never!

MITRICH: I used to work in town, for this merchant, but I spent
everything I earned on drink, so I came back to the
country. I had nowhere to live, so I hired myself out,
as a labourer. *(Yawns)* O Lord!

AKIM: What does Nikita. . . What does Nikita think he's
doing? I mean. . . What I mean is, is there really
enough work for two? How can he afford it?

ANISYA: You want to know what he's doing? Well he used to
manage the work on his own, but now, he's got other
things on his mind. So he's hired help.

MITRICH: He's got plenty of money, so what does he care?

AKIM: It's wrong. I mean, it's all wrong. Sheer laziness. It's
all wrong.

ANISYA: Yes, he's lazy, and he's spoilt.

AKIM: And just when I thought things were getting better . . .
getting better. . . Money can destroy a man. It can ruin
him.

MITRICH: They say that a dog that eats too much fat goes mad.
So how is a man who indulges himself to avoid ruin?
Drink was the ruin of me. I drank for three weeks
without stopping. I drank my last pair of breeches.
When I had nothing left, I had to stop. I promised
myself I'd never touch the stuff again. Devil take it!

AKIM: And what about your wife? What happened to your
wife?

MITRICH: Dear friend, my wife? At last she's found her vocation.
She sits begging in the taverns in town. She cuts a fine
figure. One eye gouged out, and the other black. Her
muzzle, twisted. Good luck to her! She's never sober.

AKIM: O – oh! What's going on here? What's happening? I
            mean how could you –

MITRICH: Shh! Tell me, where else is there for the wife of an old
            soldier? I'm telling you, she's found her vocation.

            Silence.

AKIM: *(To Anisya)* Nikita. . . What's he doing in town? Did
            he have something. . . I mean did he take something to
            sell?

ANISYA: *(Sits at the table and serves the food.)* He took nothing.
            He was going to get some money from the bank.

AKIM: What does he need money for? What's he going to do
            with it?

ANISYA: It's just that there are some twenty or thirty roubles
            due to us, which he's going to take out of the bank,
            because we've run a bit short.

AKIM: Take out? But if he takes out thirty now. . . And does
            the same tomorrow, and the day after and the day after
            that. . . Well, soon, there'll be nothing left.

ANISYA: It's just the interest. The money's safe.

AKIM: Safe? How can it be safe? You take some out, and
            expect me to believe it's still there? Look, if I pour
            grain, or whatever . . . into a bin. Or fill a barn. And
            then I keep taking it out . . . It's not going to stay full
            for very long, is it? They're up to something in those
            banks. They'll cheat you. Check what you've got, or
            you stand to lose. Safe indeed! You keep spending the
            money and expect me to believe it's still there.

ANISYA: Look, I don't know how it works. Ivan Moseich
            advised us. He said, "Put the money in the bank. It'll
            be safe there, and you collect the interest which is all
            extra."

MITRICH: It's true. I've worked with tradespeople, and they all do
            it. They put their money in the bank, and spend the
            rest of the time lying on the stove, living off the
            interest.

AKIM: All sounds very strange to me. I mean, how does it get there, eh? You say they collect it. . . But where does it come from, this interest? Who earns it? Where do they earn it?

ANISYA: They get it from the bank.

MITRICH: She doesn't know what she's talking about. There's no point in listening to women. What do they know? Look, let me explain it to you. Are you listening? Right. Well, let's say, that you have some money and I don't. When spring comes, I've a bare field and no seed to sow. And to make matters worse, I can't pay my taxes. So, I come to you, and I say, "Akim, lend us ten roubles. I'll pay you back in the autumn, when I've harvested my crop." Out of gratitude, I also offer to harvest a couple of acres of your crop, for nothing. Of course there's some security on the loan, as well. Just in case the harvest fails. If I can't pay you back the money, you take a cow, or my horse, or both. . . But none of this is good enough for you. You'll only agree to the loan, if I'm prepared to add two or three roubles, to the amount I pay back. What am I supposed to do? I need that money. I agree to your terms, and I take the ten roubles. In the autumn when I've made my money, I pay you ten, and you squeeze an extra three out of me.

AKIM: Dishonest peasants do this . . . I mean, this is what happens when a man strays from the path of God. It's all wrong you know.

MITRICH: Wait, let me explain how the same principle is at work in the banks. . . One stage on. Now remember you've just fleeced me for an extra three roubles. Anisya has some money, and because she's a woman she doesn't know what to do with it. She comes to you and says, "Can't you make some profit with my money?" "Certainly, I can." And you take it. You wait. . . The next spring, and I'm back, having spent all my money. I say, "Give me another ten, I'd be much obliged." You look to see if there's any flesh on me. If you can fleece me you lend me her money. But if I'm just skin and bone and can't even feed myself, then you realise there's no point in lending me the money. You say, "Sorry mate, God help you!" And you look for someone else to lend the money to. When you find that person, you lend him your money, and Anisya's. You skin him for all he's worth, and divide the profit between you. This is the way the banks work. And the money goes round and round. It's a very clever system, my friend.

AKIM: *(Getting excited.)* It can't be right! This is terrible. The peasants do this . . . I mean, the peasants behave like this. . . And they know it's a sin, but they claim they have no choice. It's against the law. You know, it's against the law. It's evil. How can educated people –

MITRICH: It's their favourite pastime. Take any woman, or a stupid man. . . If they don't know what to do with their money, they take it to the bank. And the bank is only too pleased to have it. It's their livelihood. With that money, they can fleece others. It's a very clever system.

AKIM: *(Sighs)* There's only one thing worse than not having money, and that's having too much. That's what it amounts to. God told us to work hard. But if you put money in the bank . . . fall asleep on the stove . . . lie there idle . . . and let it feed you – It's evil! It's against the law!

MITRICH: Against the law? Not any more. People with money skin the peasants to the bone.

AKIM: *(Sighs)* The times we live in . . . I mean, just take those new lavatories in town. Have you seen them? What a sight! They're all polished up. Polished up! You know, they're that smart – There's as fine a shine on them as you'd find in any inn! But what's the point? That's what I want to know. There's no point in the decoration. People forget God. They have forgotten . . . forgotten God. We forget about God . . .

         Akim leaves the table. Mitrich climbs on to the stove.

AKIM: Thank you Anisya, my dear. I'm full.

ANISYA: *(Clearing the table while still eating.)* If only the old man would speak to him, and make him see what it is he's doing to us, to himself. I'm ashamed to ask him.

AKIM: What's that?

ANISYA: Nothing. Nothing. I was talking to myself.

           Anyutka enters.

AKIM: Here's my clever little girl. Always busy, eh? You're
           cold, aren't you?

ANYUTKA: Freezing. Hello Grandpa.

ANISYA: Well? Any sign of him?

ANYUTKA: Not there. Adrian was there, and he said he'd seen
           them in town. . . In a tavern. He said Papa was drunk
           as drunk –

ANISYA: Here, have something to eat.

ANYUTKA: *(Going to the stove.)* I'm so cold. My hands are numb.

           *Akim takes off his leg wrappings and shoes, while
           Anisya washes the dishes.*

ANISYA: Father?

AKIM: What is it?

ANISYA: How's Marina?

AKIM: She's all right. She's getting along fine. She's a sensible
           woman, who gets on with life. You see, she works hard.
           She's very well. She's zealous, she's diligent and she's
           very patient. I mean, she's a fine little woman. Oh yes,
           she's getting on all right.

ANISYA: I've heard, there's been some talk in your village, that a
           relative of Marina's husband might be interested in
           Akulina. What've you heard?

AKIM: The Mironovs? Yes, the women were talking about it,
           but I'm not sure what they were saying. I don't know
           the outcome. The old women were talking about . . . I
           can't remember. My memory's going. The Mironovs?
           Well, they're good peasants. I mean, there's nothing
           wrong with them.

ANISYA: I'd like her to get married, as soon as possible.

AKIM: And why's that?

ANYUTKA: *(Who has been keeping a look-out.)* They're back.

*Enter Nikita ladened with a bundle, a bag and
numerous paper-wrapped packages. He opens the door,
and stands in the doorway.*

ANISYA: Don't take any notice of them.

She continues to wash the dishes.

NIKITA: Anisya! My wife! Look who's here?

Anisya glances at him and looks away. She's quiet.

NIKITA: *(Sternly)* Look who it is! Have you forgotten?

ANISYA: Stop showing off and come inside.

NIKITA: *(Threatening)* Who is it?

ANISYA: *(Goes to take his arm and lead him into the room).* Who
else could it be, but my husband. Come in. Come
on.

NIKITA: *(Resisting)* That's better. Husband. And what's his
name? Now make sure you pronounce it correctly.

ANISYA: Don't be so stupid, Nikita!

NIKITA: That's right. Nikita. Now, don't be grudging, let's have
his full name.

ANISYA: Akimych. Enough?

NIKITA: Akimych, that's right. And the surname!

ANISYA: *(Laughs as she pulls him into the room.)* Chilikin! Look
at the state you're in!

NIKITA: Chilikin, correct! *(Holding on to the doorpost.)* Now, can
you tell me, which foot Chilikin will put into the room
first?

ANISYA: That's enough now. You're letting in the cold.

NIKITA: Tell me! Which foot? You've got to tell me!

ANISYA: *(To herself.)* I'm bored with this. I don't know. . . The
left. Come in, will you?

NIKITA: That's right!

ANISYA: Look who's come to see you.

NIKITA: My father? I'm not ashamed of him. Let me pay him

my respects. Good evening, Papa. *(Bows and offers his hand.)* I'm so pleased to see you.

AKIM: *(Looking away.)* This is what drink does to a man. It's disgusting.

NIKITA: Drink? Yes, I can't deny it, I've had a drink with a friend. I drank his health!

ANISYA: Go and lie down!

NIKITA: Tell me, where am I?

ANISYA: You'll be all right, just go and lie down.

NIKITA: First, I'm going to have tea with my father. Start the samovar. Akulina, why don't you come in?

AKULINA: *(Enters. Smartly dressed. She is also loaded with packages. To Nikita)* You've lost everything. Where's my yarn?

NIKITA: Your yarn? It'll be there somewhere. Keep looking! Hey Mitrich! What are you doing? Gone to sleep? Well, you can go and unharness my horse!

AKIM: *(Stares at Nikita.)* How dare he. What does he think he's doing? That poor old man's exhausted. He's been working all day, and Nikita lords it, "Unharness my horse.!" Pah! It's disgraceful!

MITRICH: *(Climbs off the stove and puts on his felt boots.)* God have mercy on us! Well, where is it? In the yard? The poor creature. It'll be tired. Just look at him. Pissed out of his skull. O Lord. Blessed Nicholas the martyr, have mercy on us!

Puts on his sheepskin and goes into the yard.

NIKITA: *(Sits down.)* Forgive me Papa. It's true, I've been drinking. . . But we all have to drink, don't we? I mean even a hen has to drink, doesn't it? Please forgive me. Don't worry about Mitrich, he doesn't mind, he likes looking after my horse.

ANISYA: Shall I start the samovar?

NIKITA: My father's here, and I want to talk to him. So, we'll have some tea! *(To Akulina.)* Have you brought in all that shopping?

AKULINA: The shopping? I've brought in my things. The rest is
              still in the sledge. Here, this isn't mine.

              *She throws a package on to the table, and hides the rest in a
              large chest. Anyutka watches her intently. Akim doesn't look
              at his son, as he lays his leg wrappings and bast shoes on the
              stove.*

ANISYA: That chest was already full! What else can he have
              bought her?

NIKITA: *(Trying to appear sober.)* Papa, don't get cross at me.
              You think I'm drunk, but I'm all right. Really, I am. I
              can hold my liquor. I'm perfectly capable of having a
              sensible conversation with you. I know why you're
              here. You want some money. I remember. . . Your old
              horse . . . no good any more. . . It was worn out. You
              need another. You shall have the money, don't worry.
              Leave it to me. If we were talking about a large sum,
              then I'm afraid you'd have to wait. You shall have it.
              There, that's that!

AKIM: *(Fiddling with his leggings.)* Well son, spring is on its
              way. The thaw's started you know. It's difficult to get
              anywhere, when the thaw's on.

NIKITA: What are you talking about? The thaw? Meaning? You
              don't want to talk to me, because you think I'm drunk.
              Is that it? We'll have some tea. Look, let me just say,
              I'll give you the money. I'll see you right. Don't worry.

AKIM: *(Shaking his head.)* Ehh, ahh, ahh!

NIKITA: Here, here's the money. *(Takes a wallet out of his
              pocket, thumbs through a wadge of notes; finds a ten
              rouble note, and hands it to his father.)* Here, take it. . .
              For the horse. . . I must look after my father. Here,
              take it. I don't begrudge it you.

              Nikita thrusts the money at Akim. Akim won't take it.

NIKITA: *(Grabs Akim's arm.)* Take it! I'm giving it to you. I
              don't begrudge it you!

AKIM: No, I can't. I can't take it. I can't talk to you when
              you're in this state. You're not yourself.

NIKITA: Take it. I'm not letting you go without it.

Shoving the note in Akim's hand.

ANISYA: *(Enters)* Please take it. He won't leave you alone until you do.

AKIM: *(Takes it. Shaking his head)* Ugh, drink! The man is lost in drink. . . .

NIKITA: That's better. That's more like it. And if you repay me, you repay me. . . If not, I don't care. God be with you. I insist, I insist. . . That's that. Akulina, show us your presents!

AKULINA: What?

NIKITA: Let's see the presents!

AKULINA: Presents? Why? I've just put them away.

NIKITA: Get them out again. Anyutka would like to see what you've got. Show them to her! Unpack the shawl. And give it here.

AKIM: O – oh, it makes me sick just to look at him . . .

Climbs on to the stove.

AKULINA: *(Unpacks the chest and spreads the goods on the table.)* What's the point of looking at them?

ANYUTKA: *(Referring to the shawl.)* It's so pretty. It's like Stepanida's

AKULINA: Stepanida's? It's much nicer than hers. *(Getting excited as she unpacks the packages.)* It's good quality material. It's French –

ANYUTKA: Oh look, what beautiful chintz. Mashutka has some like that. Only I think hers has got a lighter pattern. I think the pattern's on a sky blue background. That's so pretty!

NIKITA: That's right!

Anisya is angry. She goes into the storeroom, to return seconds later with a table cloth and the chimney for the samovar. She goes to the table.

ANISYA: For heaven's sake, there's no room!

NIKITA: Anisya, just look at the stuff!

ANISYA: I've seen enough, haven't I? Take them away.

            Sweeping the shawl off the table on to the floor.

AKULINA: What d'you that for? Throw your own things on the floor!

            Picks up the shawl.

NIKITA: Anisya, look!

ANISYA: Why should I?

NIKITA: See, I haven't forgotten you. Look! *(Holds up a package for Anisya, and then sits on it.)* A present for you! But you've got to earn it. Now, all you have to do, is tell me where I'm sitting.

ANISYA: Bully! I'm not afraid of you. You just remember whose money it is that's buying you drink and presents for your flat slut! MINE!

AKULINA: Yours? You wanted to steal it, but you couldn't manage it on your own. Get out of my way!

            Trying to push past Anisya.

NIKITA: *(Coming between the two women.)* Ladies, ladies that's enough.

AKULINA: She started it. Tell her to shut up. You think people don't know about you?

ANISYA: Know what? Come on, tell me! Tell me! I'll tell you what they know –

AKULINA: They know all about you!

ANISYA: They know you're a whore, living with another woman's husband.

AKULINA: And you killed your husband!

ANISYA: *(Lunging at Akulina.)* Liar!

NIKITA: *(Restraining her.)* Anisya! What's the matter with you?

ANISYA: You want to frighten me? I'm not afraid of you!

NIKITA: Get out!

            Turning Anisya round, pushes her out of the room.

ANISYA: Where am I going? I'm not leaving my own house!

NIKITA: Get out, and stay out!

ANISYA: I'm not going. *(Weeping and shrieking; clutching at the
             doorpost as Nikita pushes her.)* What are you doing?
             You can't drive me out of my own house! What are you
             doing! You cruel bastard! You won't get away with
             this. You won't!

NIKITA: Out! Get out!

ANISYA: I'll go to the village elder. I'll go to the police!

NIKITA: Out, I said!

             Pushing her out.

ANISYA: *(Outside)* I'll kill myself!

NIKITA: You don't scare me!

ANYUTKA: O – o – oh! Poor, poor Mama!
             (Cries)

NIKITA: I'm not afraid of her. What are you crying for? She'll
             be back. Go and see to the samovar.

             Exit Anyutka.

AKULINA: *(Collects and tidies away her presents.)* The mean bitch.
             Look what she's gone and done. It's all dirty. She's
             ruined it. You wait, I'll tear her jacket to pieces! I will.
             I promise.

NIKITA: Look, I've got rid of her, isn't that enough?

AKULINA: She's made it all dirty! It was brand new! I'm telling
             you, if you hadn't thrown her out, I'd have hooked her
             eyes out!

NIKITA: Calm down, will you? What's the point in getting so
             worked up? Do you think I love her?

AKULINA: Love her? How could anyone love the bull-faced
             baggage! You should have got rid of her in the
             beginning, then none of this would've happened.
             The house and the money would have come to
             me. "I'm mistress of the house," she says. She's
             supposed to look after you. Look at the way she looked

after her last husband. She's a murderer. She'll kill
you.

NIKITA: Nothing stops a woman in full flight. You don't know
               what you're talking about.

AKULINA: I do. I can't live with her. I'll throw her out. She can't
               live with me. She's not mistress of the house. She's a
               mean, calculating selfish bitch!

NIKITA: Shut up! Look, just don't worry about her! Don't
               even look at her. Look to me. I'm master. I do what I
               like. I don't love her any more. I'm in love with you. I
               love whoever I want to. I've got the real power. She'll
               have to watch her step. I've got her where I want her!
               (Points to his feet.) Ah, it's a shame we haven't got the
               concertina. I could play. You could dance.
               (Sings)
               So long,
               As there's bread in the stove,
               And porridge on the shelf,
               We'll live.
               We'll live happily,
               'Til death comes for you and me,
               Then we'll die.
               So long,
               As there's bread in the stove,
               And porridge on the shelf,
               We'll live!

               *Mitrich enters; takes off his coat, and climbs on to the
               stove.*

MITRICH: The women have been fighting again. Scratching each
               other. Lord help us! Blessed St Nicholas have mercy
               on us . . .

AKIM: *(Still on the edge of the stove; tying up his leg wrappings,
               having put on his bast shoes.)* That's right, old man. You
               curl up in the corner, and get yourself some sleep.

MITRICH: *(Settling himself.)* The trouble is, they won't share
               anything. O Lord.

NIKITA: Let's have some brandy. We'll have it with our tea.

ANYUTKA: *(Enters. To Akulina.)* Akulina, the samovar's boiling.

NIKITA: Where's your mother?

ANYUTKA: She's in the hall. She's crying.

NIKITA: So that's what the noise is. Call her in. Tell her to bring the samovar. Akulina, you lay the table.

AKULINA: Lay the table? All right.

She does so.

NIKITA: *(Unpacks some brandy, bread rolls and salt herrings.)* This is mine. The yarn is for my wife. The paraffin is in the hall. There's some money here. . . Wait. *(Takes out an abacus.)* I'd better add this up. Straight away. *(Adds)* Wheat-flour: eighty kopecks . . . vegetable oil – ten roubles to my father. Papa, papa! Come and have some tea!

Silence. Akim doesn't move.

ANISYA: *(Enters with the samovar.)* Where shall I put it?

NIKITA: On the table. So what did the village elder have to say, eh? Come on. Come and sit down. Tell Nikita all about it. Here, come and have something to eat. Cheer up. Don't be angry. What's there to be angry about? Sit down. Have a drink. *(Passing her a glass.)* Here, I've bought you a present.

He gives her the parcel he's been sitting on. Anisya takes it in silence, shaking her head.

AKIM: *(Gets up, puts on his coat, goes to the table and puts down the ten rouble note.)* It's your money, you keep it!

NIKITA: *(Doesn't see the money.)* Why've you put your coat on? Where are you going?

AKIM: I'm going. . . I'm going now. Christ forgive us our sins. *(Picks up his cap and belt.)*

NIKITA: What? Where are you going at this time of night?

AKIM: I can't stay . . . I mean I can't stay. . . Not in this house. . . I can't stay. . . Forgive me!

NIKITA: You're not going anywhere, before you've had your tea.

AKIM: *(Tying on his belt.)* I'm going . . . because . . . well, I

don't like it here. Nikita, I don't like it here. . . Here in
this house, I mean. The life you lead – Bad. . . It's all
wrong. Now, I must go.

NIKITA: What d'you mean? Tell me! Sit down and have some
tea!

ANISYA: Father, if you leave now, imagine what people will say.
They'll think we've offended you.

AKIM: I'm not offended. . . Not at all. I mean, I'm not
offended. It's just that my son . . . that my son –
Ruin. . . Is on the road to ruin.

NIKITA: To ruin? What d'you mean?

AKIM: Ruin. Ruin. Your life is in ruins. Remember what I
said to you last summer?

NIKITA: You said all sorts of things.

AKIM: I spoke to you about . . . about . . . well, you know that
orphan you mistreated . . . that girl . . . Marina. . . You
wronged her.

NIKITA: Oh don't start. That's all in the past. All over.

AKIM: *(Getting excited.)* Over? No, that's it. . . It's not. Over,
I mean. One sin leads to another . . . to another. . . To
sin again and again, until you're caught in a web of sin.

NIKITA: Sit and drink your tea. Not another word out of you.

AKIM: I can't. . . I don't feel like it. I'm sick. You've made
me sick. I feel wretched. I don't feel like any tea.

NIKITA: Ah, you're rambling again. Sit down.

AKIM: You're caught in a web of sin. A man must have a soul,
Nikita. A soul.

NIKITA: Look, what right have you to insult me in my own
home? Why d'you keep on at me? I'm not a child. I'm
a grown-up.

AKIM: What I'm saying, is that it's no good. It's too late.
You're on the road to ruin.

NIKITA: *(Angry)* We manage perfectly well! We don't come
begging to you. You come to us!

AKIM: For money? You can keep your money. I'd rather be a beggar . . . be a beggar, than take it off you!

NIKITA: Papa stop it! Why are you so angry? Why spoil the party?

Restraining his father by the arm.

AKIM: *(Screams)* Let go of me! I'm not staying! I'd rather spend the night in the open, curled up under some fence, than in this place. Bah! God forgive me!

Exit.

NIKITA: What was all that about?

AKIM: *(Poking his head round the door.)* You must pull yourself together, Nikita! A man must have a soul!

Exit.

AKULINA: *(Arranging the glasses.)* Shall I pour the tea?

All silent.

MITRICH: Ah, Lord have mercy on me, a poor sinner!

All start.

NIKITA: *(Lies on the bench.)* I'm so bored. I'm bored with life. Akulina, where's the concertina?

AKULINA: Your concertina? You took it be mended, remember? I've poured you some tea. Drink it.

NIKITA: I don't want it. Turn the lights out. I'm bored. I'm so bored.

Weeps.

END OF ACT THREE

ACT FOUR

Autumn. Evening. A courtyard. The moon shines. At the back, centre, the hall of Piotr's cottage. On the right the warmest part of the house (used in the winter); on the left the coldest part (only used during the summer). People talking, and drunken cries, from within. A neighbour comes out of the hall and beckons to Anisya's friend, Mavra.

NEIGHBOUR: Where's Akulina? Why can't she be here? What's happened to her?

MAVRA: She'd love to be here, but she's not well. All her suitor's relatives have turned up. They all want to see her. But the poor girl is lying in the coldest part of the house, and won't move.

NEIGHBOUR: What's wrong with her?

MAVRA: They say the evil eye has lighted on her belly.

NEIGHBOUR: You mean –

MAVRA: Don't say it.

NEIGHBOUR: Well. . . Such sin. The matchmaker, and all the bridegroom's relatives are bound to find out.

MAVRA: No. They're all too drunk. The only thing they're worried about is the size of the dowry. By the way, have you heard, it's very good. It includes two fur coats, my dear; six dresses, a French shawl and I don't know how much linen! As for the money. . . They say as much as two hundred roubles comes –

NEIGHBOUR: It doesn't matter what the dowry's worth, he'll never be happy when everyone finds out what's happened.

MAVRA: Shhh! Here comes his father.

Ivan comes out of the hall, hiccoughing. Neighbour and Mavra withdraw within.

IVAN: I'm pouring sweat. It's so hot in there. I must have some fresh air. *(Stands panting.)* There's something not right here – I'm not happy – There's something wrong. . . Ah, here comes the old woman.

MATRIONA: *(Entering from the hall.)* I was wondering where you'd got to. I said to myself, "Where's he gone? Where's the groom's father?" And here you are. My dear man, we must thank God that everything is going so well. Far be it from me to boast, but I am responsible for this match. You know, I wouldn't know how to boast, but let me just say one thing: I'm sure you can appreciate how well everything's going. I'm sure you'll be grateful to me, for years to come. The bride, you know, is something special. You won't find another like her in the whole district.

IVAN: I'm sure you're right. And the money –

MATRIONA: Don't worry about the money. She's still got the money her father left her. That's a hundred and fifty roubles. Not to be sneezed at!

IVAN: Oh, I'm not complaining. But you know how it is. . . He's our son, and we want what's best for him.

MATRIONA: Let me tell you something. If it hadn't been for me, you'd never have found her. The Karmilins made an offer, but I said "No, we can do better." Look, let me tell you something about the money. I can see you're worried. The truth of the matter is, that when her father, God rest his soul, was dying, he gave orders for his widow to take Nikita in – Believe me, I know all about it from my son. He also gave orders, that the money should go to Akulina. Well, someone else, you know, would have wanted that money for themselves. But my Nikita gave it all to Akulina. Now, that's a lot of money . . .

IVAN: But I've heard that there was more money than is being offered. I've heard that your son's on the make.

MATRIONA: My dear man, the grass is always greener on the other side. Stop worrying. Let's settle this business, once and for all. She's a wonderful girl. As pretty as a daisy.

IVAN: I'm sure. But there's just one thing my wife and I were wondering. . . Why won't she show herself? I mean if she's the sickly type, well we'll have to re –

MATRIONA: O – oh! Sickly? There isn't a healthier girl in the whole district. Her flesh is so firm, I defy you to pinch it. You saw her the other day, didn't you? I mean, she's a terrific worker. It's true, she's a little deaf. But one worm hole doesn't spoil the apple. The reason why she hasn't shown herself today is that someone has cast a spell on her. I know the bitch that's done it. She only had to hear that Akulina was getting married and she cast a spell. But I know a cure. She'll be up tomorrow, don't worry!

IVAN: In that case, let's agree. It's a deal.

MATRIONA: That's what I like to hear. Now don't go changing your mind, will you? And you won't forget me. . . I've worked so hard for this. Don't forget me in my hour of need.

> *Woman's voice off: "If we're going, let's go! Come on Ivan!"*

IVAN: I'm coming!

> *The guests, who are all getting ready to leave, crowd into the hall.*

ANYUTKA: *(Running out of the hall, beckoning to Anisya.)* Mama!

ANISYA: *(Doesn't move.)* What is it?

ANYUTKA: Mama, over here, or they'll hear us.

> *They move to one side, by the barn.*

ANISYA: Well? What's the matter? Where's Akulina?

ANYUTKA: She's in the barn. I'm so frightened. She's in a terrible state. I promise you, she is. "No," she says, "I'm in agony. I'm going to scream." Honestly, that's what she said.

ANISYA: She'll have to wait. We must say goodbye to the guests.

ANYUTKA: Oh Mama, but she's in so much pain. And she's so angry. "It's no good them drinking my health," she says, "I'm not going to get married," she says. "I'm going to die." Mama, what if she dies? Mama it will be terrible if my sister dies. Mama, I'm so frightened.

ANISYA: Don't worry, she's not going to die. Just keep well away from her.

They leave.

MITRICH: *(Enters through the gate. He starts to rake the straw.)* O Lord, Blessed St Nicholas. . . . They drink so much. How the smell gets everywhere. It lingers, I can smell it out here. But no, not me. I don't touch the stuff. Look what a mess they've made of the straw. It'd be quite different if they had to eat it. Look, there's hardly any left. *(Pointing to the remains of a bundle of straw.)* The smell out here is awful. My nose is full of it. To hell with the lot of them. *(Yawns)* It's time I had a lie down. I daren't go inside. That smell haunts me. It's dreadful.

The sound of the guests leaving.

MITRICH: Well, it sounds like they're off. O Lord, Blessed St Nicholas. . . One minute they're hugging each other, enjoying themselves and the next – Those are empty gestures.

NIKITA: *(Enters)* Mitrich, go and lie down. I'll rake the straw.

MITRICH: Whatever you say. Give it to the sheep. All the guests have gone, then?

NIKITA: Yes. This is all wrong. . . I don't know what to do.

MITRICH: A ghastly business. Look, why does she have to have it here? Why not the Foundlings' Hospital? They'll look after anything you give them. And it doesn't matter how many. No questions asked. Nothing said. They'll even pay the mother to work as a wet nurse. Nowadays it couldn't be easier.

NIKITA: I don't care what you think.

MITRICH: Why should I bother. Of course, you know what's best. Ugh, you reek of alcohol. I'm going inside. *(Goes inside, yawning.)* O Lord –

Nikita sits on a sledge. Long silence.

NIKITA: I hate this life.

ANISYA: *(Enters from the hall.)* Where are you?

NIKITA: Over here.

ANISYA: What are you doing? Come on, there's no time to waste. We must get rid of it.

NIKITA: What are we going to do?

ANISYA: Just do as I say.

NIKITA: Look, if you took mother and child to the Foundlings' Home –

ANISYA: If that's what you want, you take them! Look, you fucked her, but you're too weak to accept the consequences.

NIKITA: What do you want me to do?

ANISYA: Go down into the cellar and dig a hole –

NIKITA: Can't you women think of some other way?

ANISYA: *(Mimicks him.)* "Think of some other way. . ." No we can't. You ought to have thought about it a year ago. I've told you what to do. Now get on with it.

NIKITA: I hate this!

ANYUTKA: *(Enters)* Mama! Grandma's calling for you. My sister's had her baby. Honest. I heard it cry.

ANISYA: The Devil take you! You're lying! It was kittens squealing. Go straight to bed, before I hit you!

ANYUTKA: Please Mama, it's true. I promise you.

ANISYA: *(Raising a hand to her.)* What did I say? Get out of my sight!

Anyutka rushes out.

ANISYA: *(To Nikita.)* Go on. Do as you're told.

Exit.

Long pause.

NIKITA: I hate my life. What a ghastly mess. These women – They're nothing but trouble. "You should have thought about it a year ago. . ." Is there ever time to think beforehand? Last summer, what was I supposed to think about, when Anisya fell in love with me? What could I do? Should I've behaved like a monk? The

master died, and I made good my sin, which was the
proper thing to do. I'm sure I'm not the only one it's
happened to. The powders were nothing to do with me.
Did I connive with her? If I'd known what the bitch
was doing, I'd have killed her right there and then. Just
to get her out of the way. . . . And then the cunning
hag had to make sure I was involved in her dirty work.
From that moment, I've hated her. As soon as Mama
told me what had happened, I started to hate her. Hate her.
I can't bear the sight of her. How was I supposed to
live with her? And then. . . . Well, Akulina started to
fall for me. Well, what was I supposed to do? If it
hadn't have been me, it would've been someone else.
The result – this mess. But what has happened, none of
it is my fault. *(Thinking)* These women are so fearless.
They've conceived a terrible plan. I want nothing to do
with it.

Enter Matriona with a lantern and spade.

MATRIONA: Why are you sitting there like a wet hen? What did she
tell you to do? Get on with it.

NIKITA: What about you?

MATRIONA: We know what we're doing. Now, you just do as you're
told, and do your bit.

NIKITA: You're determined to involve me in this.

MATRIONA: What? You're not thinking of backing out now, are
you? To get this far and then give up?

NIKITA: But think what it is you're doing. It's a living soul!

MATRIONA: A living soul? It's barely alive. What are we supposed
to do with it? If we take it to the Foundlings' Home,
it'll die anyway. And it won't take long for the rumours
to start. You know what people are, they talk, talk, and
Akulina will end up staying here.

NIKITA: But what happens if they find out?

MATRIONA: We can do what we like in our own home. There'll be
no trace of it. Do as you're told. Come on. We need
you. We need a man's help. Take the spade and go into
the cellar. I'll hold the lantern.

NIKITA: Then what do I do?

MATRIONA: *(Whispers)* Dig a hole. Then we'll fetch it, and we'll
               bury it. Quick. She's calling me again. Get down there.
               I must go!

NIKITA: Is it dead?

MATRIONA: Yes. Quick, quick! Some people still haven't gone to
               bed. You know what people are like, they hear
               something, they see something. . . They have to know
               what's going on! A policeman came by this evening.
               Here take it. *(Giving him the spade.)* Go down into the
               cellar, and dig the hole in the corner, where the ground
               is soft, so it can be easily put back. Mother Earth can
               keep a secret. She won't tell anyone. She'll lick it clean
               with her tongue. Go on. There's a good boy, go on!

NIKITA: No, I'm not going to. To hell with you! If you're so
               keen, do it yourself!

ANISYA: *(From the doorway.)* Has he done it?

MATRIONA: What are you doing? Where is it?

ANISYA: I've wrapped it in rags. No one will hear it. Has he dug
               the hole?

MATRIONA: He doesn't want to.

ANISYA: *(Stepping forward, full of rage.)* Doesn't want to, eh? So
               you'd prefer the prison, would you? Food for the rats!
               I'm going to tell the policeman everything! Right now!
               We'll die together! I'll tell him everything!

NIKITA: *(Panic stricken.)* What will you tell him?

ANISYA: What'll I tell him? I'll tell him everything. Who took
               the money? You did!

               Nikita silent.

ANISYA: And who poisoned my husband? I did! But you knew.
               You knew! I conspired with you!

MATRIONA: Shut up! Dearest Nikita, why are you being so
               obstinate? What are we supposed to do now? We must
               finish the job. Go on my darling. Go and dig the hole.

ANISYA: Look at him. He's so innocent. "He doesn't want to."

Well, you've bullied me for too long. You've trampled me underfoot. Now it's my turn. You do as you're told, or I'll tell everything. Take that spade.

NIKITA: Why can't you leave me alone?! *(He holds the spade, but hesitates.)* I don't see why I should have to, if I don't want to. I'm not going to dig the hole.

ANISYA: You're what? *(Screams)* Everybody come here! Come here! Everybody here!

MATRIONA: *(Putting her hand over Anisya's mouth.)* What's the matter with you? Have you gone mad? He'll do it. . . Go on, Nikita. . . There's a good boy. . . Go on –

ANISYA: Everybody come here!

NIKITA: Shut up! You stupid woman. If we're going to do it, let's get on with it. *(He walks towards the cellar.)*

MATRIONA: That's right, if you fool around you must cover your tracks.

ANISYA: *(Still agitated.)* He and his slut have taunted me for too long. I've had enough. I'm not going to be the only one. Let him know what it's like to be a murderer.

MATRIONA: There, there, now calm down. . . Don't go getting excited. Let's do things quietly, one thing at a time. Now you go back to Akulina. I'm sure he'll do his bit.

Matriona follows Nikita to the cellar with the lantern. Nikita climbs down into the cellar.

ANISYA: I'll make him strangle the filthy brat! *(Still excited.)* I've had to suffer, alone, with Piotr's bones pricking my conscience. Let him find out what it's like. I'll make sure – I'll make sure he knows what it's like!

NIKITA: *(In the cellar.)* Give me some light!

MATRIONA: *(Holding up the light. To Anisya.)* He's digging. Go and get it.

ANISYA: Keep an eye on him, he's bound to try and escape. He's such a coward. I'll go and get it.

MATRIONA: Don't forget to baptize it. Or I'll do it myself if you've got a cross?

ANISYA: I'll find one. I know what to do.

Exit.

THERE IS AN ALTERNATIVE ENDING TO
THIS ACT ACCORDING TO THE
INSTRUCTIONS OF THE RUSSIAN CENSOR
IN 1895. SEE PAGES 93–101.

MATRIONA: She gets herself into such a state. I know what a
difficult time she's had, but – Ah well, God willing,
when this business is over, things'll settle down. We'll
get rid of the girl without any fuss. My son'll live in
peace. Thanks be to God, they won't want for
anything. And they'll never forget me. Where would
the pair of them be, without Matriona? They wouldn't
have known what to do. *(Looking into the cellar.)* How
are you getting on?

NIKITA: *(Climbs up: only his head is visible.)* What are you
doing? What are you waiting for? If we're to do it, let's
get it over quickly.

*Matriona makes her way to the hall and meets Anisya
coming out. Anisya holds the baby, wrapped in rags.*

MATRIONA: Well? Did you baptize it?

ANISYA: Yes. But it was all I could do to get it off her. She
clung to it for dear life. Here take it! *(Crosses to the
cellar and holds out the baby for Nikita to take.)*

NIKITA: *(Doesn't take it.)* You take it down.

ANISYA: I said, take it! *(Throws the child at him.)*

NIKITA: *(Catches it.)* It's still alive! Mama, it's moving. It's
alive. What do I do?

ANISYA: *(Snatches the baby off him, and throws it into the cellar.)*
Hurry up! Smother it! It'll soon die! *(Pushes Nikita into
the cellar.)* It's your mistake, you get rid of it!

MATRIONA: *(Sitting on a step.)* He's too gentle. I know it's hard on
him, poor boy. But we've no alternative. It's his fault.

*Anisya stands over the cellar entrance. Matriona looks
on, and reflects on the situation.*

MATRIONA: He's so frightened. However cruel it may seem . . . we've no alternative. Where else could it go? And to think that there are people desperate for children. They pray to God, and he won't answer their prayers. Or perhaps their children are born – still-born. Dead. Take the wife of our local priest, for example. . . Here it's not wanted and it lives! He must've finished by now. *(To Anisya.)* Well?

ANISYA: *(Looking into the cellar.)* He's put a board over it. He's sat on the board. He's finished!

MATRIONA: O – oh! If only we didn't have to sin. It can't be helped.

NIKITA: *(Emerges from the cellar, shaking.)* It's still alive! I can't! I can't! It's still alive!

ANISYA: If it's still alive, where do you think you're going?

Attempting to stop him.

NIKITA: *(Rushing at her.)* Get off! I'll kill you! *(He grabs her arm; she breaks free; he charges her with the spade; Matriona steps between them; Anisya runs to the porch as Matriona wrestles with Nikita to get the spade off him. To Matriona.)* I'll kill you! I'll kill you as well. Get out! *(Matriona runs to Anisya. Nikita stays put.)* I'll kill you. I'll kill you. All of you!

MATRIONA: He's so scared. The poor boy's scared. He'll calm down in a bit –

NIKITA: What've I done? What've you made me do? It cried. As its little bones crunched under me. What've you done to me? It's alive! Honestly, it's alive! *(Silence as he listens.)* Still alive. . . Listen to its little cry – crying . . . there . . . listen! I can hear it! *(Runs back to the cellar.)*

MATRIONA: *(To Anisya.)* He's gone back. He'll bury it now. Nikita, you'll need some light.

NIKITA: *(Doesn't answer her. He listens at the cellar door.)* Nothing. I can't hear anything. I must've imagined it. *(He turns away and then stops abruptly.)* But the crunching sound of those tiny fragile bones . . . Krr

... Krrr ... Krrrrr! What've you done to me? *(He listens.)* There – There it is again! Crying. It's wailing. What is it? Mama! Mama! *(He goes to Matriona.)*

MATRIONA: My dear child, what's the matter?

NIKITA: Mama, dear Mama, I can't bear this any more. I can't do it. Mama have pity on me!

MATRIONA: I know, I know, my baby, you're so frightened. Come and have a little drink. A drink'll give you the strength to –

NIKITA: No Mama, no! No more! What've you done to me? The sound of the little bones . . . and the wailing. Never stops! Mama, what've you made me do?

Sits on the sledge.

MATRIONA: Come on. Come and have a drink. It'll do you good. The night has frightened you, but it won't last forever. No. Dawn will come. A day or two will pass . . . you won't think about it. The girl will get married, and you'll forget her. Come on, have a drink, while I sort things out in the cellar.

NIKITA: If there's any drink left, I'll finish it all!

Exit.

Anisya who is standing by the door lets Nikita pass in silence.

MATRIONA: Come on my dear, let's get to work. I'll bury it myself. Where did he put that spade? *(She finds the spade and is halfway down the cellar stairs.)* Anisya, hold the light for me!

ANISYA: What's the matter with him?

MATRIONA: Just frightened. You were too hard on him. Leave him alone, he'll be all right. God help him. Now I'll have to do the job myself. Put the lantern down there, so I can see what I'm doing.

She disappears into the cellar.

ANISYA: *(Shouts after Nikita.)* No more playing around! You were so full of yourself, you wait and see. . . Now you

know what it feels like, you won't act so high and
mighty.

*Nikita rushes out of the hall and heads straight for the
cellar.*

NIKITA: Mama! Mama!

MATRIONA: *(Emerging from the cellar.)* What is it?

NIKITA: *(Stops to listen.)* Don't bury it. It's alive! Can't you
hear it? It's alive! It's crying. There . . . There . . .
There . . . I can hear it so clearly.

MATRIONA: How could it possibly be crying. You squashed it flat.
Flat as a pancake. You crushed the head.

NIKITA: Then what is it? *(Blocking his ears.)* Still crying! My
life's ruined. I'm lost. What've they done to me? What
can I do? Where will I go?

Sits weeping on the steps to the cellar.

END OF ACT FOUR

ACT FIVE

SCENE ONE

The threshing yard. In the foreground a stack-stand; on the left, the threshing floor and on the right a barn. The barn doors are open and there is straw scattered around the entrance. In the background the farmyard and outbuildings. Singing and the tinkle of tambourines. Two girls are walking along a path, past the barn, on their way to the cottage.

GIRL 1 :   We're here, and there's hardly a mark on our boots. If we'd taken the road through the village, we'd be covered in mud.

> *The girls stop to wipe their feet on some straw. They see something.*

What's that over there?

GIRL 2 :   That's Mitrich. He's their old farm hand. It looks like he's drunk.

GIRL 1 :   I thought he didn't drink?

GIRL 2 :   Well, he's started again, hasn't he?

GIRL 1 :   Look at him. He must've been on his way to get some straw. Look, he's still got the rope in his hand. He must've fallen over, and gone fast asleep.

GIRL 2 :   They're still singing the wedding songs, which means they haven't yet been blessed. You know what they say? They say that Akulina didn't wail.

GIRL 1 :   My mother said that she didn't want to get married. That she'd never have consented if her stepfather hadn't threatened her. You know what they say about her?

> *Enter Marina, she walks past the two girls.*

MARINA :   Hello. You well?

GIRLS :   Hello Marina.

MARINA :   Are you going to the wedding?

GIRL 1:   I think it's nearly over. I just wanted to have a look.

MARINA: Would you do me a favour? Be so kind as to tell my
              husband that I'm waiting for him. Simon from Zuyev.
              You know who I mean, don't you?

GIRL 1:   Of course we do. He's related to the bridegroom isn't
              he?

MARINA: Yes. The bridegroom is his nephew.

GIRL 2:   Why don't you go? Surely you don't want to miss the
              wedding.

MARINA: I'm not in the mood for a wedding. I don't have
              the time. We've got to get going. We didn't really mean
              to stop for the wedding. We were carting oats to town,
              when we stopped to feed the horses. There, they
              insisted that we go to the wedding.

GIRL 1:   Where did you stop? At Fedorich's?

MARINA: That's right. Now, could you go and get him, I'll wait
              for you here. Tell him his wife wants to go home, and
              that the horses have been harnessed and are ready to
              leave.

GIRL 1:   Well all right – if you won't go yourself.

              *Girls go towards the cottage. Songs and the beating of
              tambourines as they go.*

MARINA: *(Assessing the situation.)* I should've gone. I don't want
              to. I haven't seen him since he rejected me. That's
              over a year ago now. I'd like to see how he lives with
              Anisya. People say they don't get on. She's a tough
              woman. I've heard she's always got to get her own way.
              I'm sure there have been times when he's thought of
              me. All he wanted was an easy life. He gave me up for
              – God help him. I bear him no grudge. It hurt at the
              time. I'll never again feel such pain. It's worn off now
              . . . forgotten. I'd like just to see him again. *(Looks
              towards the cottage and sees him.)* It's him. What's he
              doing here? Did they tell him I was here? Why's he
              left the guests? He looks so unhappy. I must go.

              *Nikita enters with his head down; swinging his arms
              from side to side, and muttering incoherently.*

NIKITA: *(Catching sight of Marina.)* Marina! Dear friend! Dearest Marina! What are you doing here?

MARINA: I'm waiting for my husband.

NIKITA: Why don't you come to the wedding. It'll be fun.

MARINA: I'm not in the mood. I'm here to fetch my husband.

NIKITA: Dearest Marina . . . *(He tries to embrace her.)*

MARINA: *(Pushing him off.)* Stop it. That's over. All past. I've come to fetch my husband. He's inside, isn't he?

NIKITA: Come on. . . not even for old time's sake? You don't want to?

MARINA: What's the point? What's past is past!

NIKITA: Just once more?

MARINA: No. Why are you here? Why have you left your guests?

NIKITA: *(Sits down in the straw.)* You want to know why I'm here? If only you knew. My life's a mess, Marina. It's so bad, I wish I were blind. I left the table. I walked out. . . To get away from all those people. If only I didn't have to see anyone, ever again.

MARINA: *(Coming closer.)* Why?

NIKITA: I can't eat, can't drink . . . can't sleep. I'm sick of this life. So sick of it. And what makes me feel worse is to know that I am totally alone. That there's no one to share my pain.

MARINA: Everyone has their own pain. Tears rinse pain away. In the past I've cried and cried.

NIKITA: Your pain belongs to your past. Now it's my turn to suffer.

MARINA: But what's wrong?

NIKITA: I'm fed up with my life. I hate myself. If only you had stayed with me. Now both our lives are ruined. Life isn't worth living.

MARINA: *(Stands by the barn and weeps. She pulls herself together.)* I can't complain, Nikita. God grant everyone as good a life as mine. I mustn't complain. When I got married, I told my husband everything. He forgave me. He doesn't reproach me. He's a humble old man. He's very fond of me. I look after his children and he's very kind to me. I'm happy with my lot. God intended it to happen like this. What's the point in complaining. How could there be anything wrong with your life? You're rich.

NIKITA: My life? If I didn't think it'd spoil the party, I'd get a rope. . . This one here – *(Picks up a rope from the straw.)* I'd chuck it over that beam; tie a noose, walk the beam, put my head in the noose and jump! That's how much I value my life.

MARINA: Don't talk like this. Christ have mercy on you.

NIKITA: You think I'm joking, don't you? You think I'm drunk? I'm not drunk. Drink doesn't affect me any more. I'm thoroughly miserable. The pain is eating me alive. I don't care about anything any more. But Marina, remember. . . Just remember the nights we spent together . . . by the railway. . . See the moon –

MARINA: Don't Nikita! Don't! It still hurts. I'm married, and so are you. My sin has been forgiven. Don't rake up the past.

NIKITA: What am I going to do? Who can I turn to?

MARINA: You know what to do. You've got a wife. Look after her, and don't lust after other women. Once upon a time you loved Anisya. Go on loving her.

NIKITA: Not Anisya. . . She's gall and wormwood to me. She's strangling me like rank weeds.

MARINA: She's still your wife. There's no point talking to you. Get back to your guests. Tell my husband I'm waiting for him.

NIKITA: If only you knew the whole story. . . But as you say, there's no point in talking.

Enter Anyutka and Marina's husband, redfaced and drunk.

MARINA'S
HUSBAND: Marina! Where's my Missis! Marina, where are you?

NIKITA: He's calling you. Your husband's coming. You'd better
             go.

MARINA: What about you?

NIKITA: Me? I'll just lie down for a while.

MARINA'S
HUSBAND: I wonder where she can have got to.

ANYUTKA: There she is! There she is, uncle! Over there by the
             barn!

MARINA'S
HUSBAND: What are you doing over there? Come to the wedding!
             The hosts want you there. Do them the honour. The
             wedding party is about to leave. As soon as they've left,
             we can go.

MARINA: *(Going to her husband.)* Please, I don't want to go to the
             wedding.

MARINA'S
HUSBAND: Come on. I'm telling you to come! You'll drink a toast.
             A toast to that rascal nephew of mine, or they'll be
             offended. Don't worry, we'll get the work done.

             *Marina's husband puts his arm around his wife and
             they stagger out.*

NIKITA: *(Sits)* I wish I hadn't seen her again, I feel worse than
             ever. The only real life I ever had was with her. And I
             threw it all away. My whole life has been a waste. *(Lies
             down.)* What am I supposed to do? If only Mother
             Earth would open, and swallow me up.

ANYUTKA: *(Sees Nikita, and runs to him.)* Papa! Papa! They're
             waiting for you. Everybody else has given their
             blessing. . . Even Godfather! Everybody, I promise
             you. Now, everybody's starting to get annoyed, because
             they're waiting for you.

NIKITA: *(To himself.)* What am I supposed to do?

ANYUTKA: What?

NIKITA: Nothing. Nothing. Don't keep bothering me.

ANYUTKA: Papa, come on! *(Nikita is silent as Anyutka tugs at his*

arm.) Papa, you must come and give your blessing.
They're so cross, I promise you. They're grumbling.

NIKITA: (*Pulling his arm free.*) Leave me alone!

ANYUTKA: Please Papa! Come on!

NIKITA: (*Threatens her with the rope.*) Go away, or I'll whip
             you –

ANYUTKA: I'm going to get Mama!

             Runs out.

NIKITA: (*Stands*) How can I? How can I hold the Holy Icon in
             my hands? How can I look her in the eye, and give her
             my blessing? (*Falls down.*) If only the earth would swallow
             me up. They'd never find me, I'd never have to see any
             of them, ever again! (*Stands*) I won't go. . . No! To hell
             with them. (*Taking off his boots, picking up a rope, tying
             a noose. He puts the noose around his neck.*) This is it!

             *Matriona enters. Nikita sees her, removes the noose
             and lies down again.*

MATRIONA: (*In a hurry.*) Nikita! Nikita! Oh, there you are. Didn't
             you hear me calling? What's the matter with you?
             Drunk? Come on darling. . . Come on, they're tired of
             waiting for you.

NIKITA: Look what you've done to me. Who am I?

MATRIONA: What's the matter? Dear boy, come on. . . Come and
             give your blessing. It's right and proper that you
             should. Then it'll all be over. Come on, the guests are
             waiting!

NIKITA: But how can I give my blessing?

MATRIONA: The usual way. You know the procedure, don't you?

NIKITA: Of course I know the procedure! But how can I, after
             what I've done to her?

MATRIONA: What've you done to her? Look, what's past is past.
             Now's not the time to worry about that. Look, nobody
             knows, from the cat to the priest, not a soul! Besides,
             the girl wants to get married!

NIKITA: How do you know she wants to?

MATRIONA: I know she's afraid. But she's going to go through with it. What else can she do? It's too late for her to change her mind. Too late. His parents are satisfied. They've met her twice, and think it's a perfect match. And they're more than happy with the money. Everything is going according to plan.

NIKITA: But what's in the cellar?

MATRIONA: In the cellar? Cabbages, mushrooms and potatoes. Nothing else. Look, forget the past.

NIKITA: If only I could. But I can't. The slightest little thing reminds me. It still haunts me. I can hear it! There! There! What've you done to me?

MATRIONA: What's the matter with you?

NIKITA: *(Face down in the straw.)* Mama, don't torture me! I can't take any more.

MATRIONA: You must give the blessing! You know what people are like. They'll start to talk: The stepfather suddenly disappears. . . He's nowhere to be found. . . He won't give his blessing. . . . They'll put two and two together. If you don't go through with this, they'll guess straight away. Nobody suspects the thief who walks through the front door. If you run from a wolf, the chances are you'll be mauled by a bear. Come on now, look the part. Don't appear frightened or they'll suspect you.

NIKITA: You got me into this mess –

MATRIONA: That's enough now. Come and give the blessing. Just do what you have to do, and that'll be that.

NIKITA: *(Still face down.)* I can't.

MATRIONA: *(To herself.)* What's happened to him? Everything was going so smoothly, and suddenly he starts behaving like this. He's obviously bewitched. Nikita get up! Look, Anisya's had to leave the party!

ANISYA: *(Enters, smartly dressed and flushed with drink.)* Mother, it's going so well! Everybody's enjoying themselves. Where is he?

MATRIONA: He's here. Lying in the straw, my dear. He must be tired. He won't move.

NIKITA: *(Turns to look at Anisya.)* Look at her! Drunk! It makes me sick to look at her! I can't live with her! *(Face down in the straw.)* One day, I'll kill her. I am so steeped in evil, things can only get worse.

ANISYA: Look at him, he's all covered in straw! Had too much to drink? *(Laughs)* I'd like to cuddle up beside you. . . Oh! There isn't time! Come on, I'll show you the way. They're all having such fun. It's lovely to see them enjoying themselves. The concertina is playing away. . . The women are singing. . . It's so beautiful. And everybody's drunk. It's just as it should be.

NIKITA: What is?

ANISYA: The wedding. It's so lively. People are already saying they've never known a wedding like it. It's just as it should be. Come on, we'll go together. I'm a bit tipsy, but I know the way.

   Takes his arm.

NIKITA: *(Pulls away, disgusted.)* You go ahead! I'll follow.

ANISYA: What's the matter with you? You're so irritable. Our problems are over. We've got rid of the one thing that came between us. The girl is out of the way! We can enjoy ourselves. Like old times. Everything is going according to plan, and it's all legal. I can't tell you how happy I am. It's as if I was marrying you again! *(Laughs)* Everybody's delighted. Everybody's grateful. They're all such wonderful people. There's old Ivan Moseich, and the policeman, singing our praises!

NIKITA: Well, what are you doing here? Go and join them.

ANISYA: Yes I will. I must get back. It must seem a bit strange . . . as if the hosts have forgotten their guests. A bit rude, when the guests are such lovely people. Come on!

NIKITA: *(Stands, and brushes the straw off himself.)* You go. I'll follow.

MATRIONA: Look at that! He listens to her, when he wouldn't listen to me!

   Matriona and Anisya turn to go.

MATRIONA: *(Turning back.)* You are coming, aren't you?

NIKITA: I'm coming. Go on. I'll follow. I'll be there to give the blessing.

The women hesitate.

NIKITA: Go on! I'm coming!

The women leave. Nikita watches them go. Sits down and removes his boots again.

I'll follow. . . Like hell I will. And when you come looking for me. . . Look no further than this beam. . . I'll hang here . . . with the noose tight around my neck. This is where you'll find me. This rope has been waiting here for me. *(Ponders)* They think I'll get over it. . . That I'll forget. No. Not this time. This time it's different. The pain. I feel it here . . . here in the heart. A wound too deep to heal. *(Looks towards the cottage.)* She's coming back. *(Mimicks Anisya.)* "I'd like to cuddle up beside you. . ." Ugh, filthy hag! The next time you hug me, will be to hold me still while they untie the knot. A last hug! *(Grabs the rope, and pulls it.)*

MITRICH: *(Sits up and clings to the rope, drunk.)* No, you're not having it! I'm not giving it to anyone. I'll fetch some. I said I'd do it, so I'll do it. I'll fetch some more straw. Is that you Nikita? *(Laughs)* The devil it is! Have you come for some straw?

NIKITA: Give me the rope!

MITRICH: No. I said no, and I mean it. Ah Nikita, you're a fool. . . As foolish as a pig's belly button. *(Laughs)* I love you, but you're a fool. You think I've been drinking, don't you? Well, to hell with you! Don't think I need you! Me, I'm a non – a non. . . You couldn't say it either! A non-commissioned officer in Her Majesty's very first Regiment of Grenadiers. I've served my Tsar and country with the greatest loyalty. But now, who am I? Who am I really? You think I'm a soldier, don't you? A fighting man? I'm not. I'm not a soldier. I'm hardly what you'd call a man. I'm an orphan, a stray. I vowed I wouldn't drink. And now I've started to smoke!
Well, don't think I'm afraid of you, because I'm not!

Nobody scares me! When I drink, I drink! Now I'll
drink for two whole weeks, non-stop! I'll pawn
everything except my cross. I'll spend all the money on
drink. I'll drink my hat. I'll pawn my passport! And
I'm not afraid of anyone!
The regiment used to flog me – To keep me off the
drink. They whipped me. Whipped me! "Well," they
said, "are you going to stop?" "No!" I said. I
mean, why should they put the fear of God in me? I am
who I am. I am as God made me. I vowed I wouldn't
touch the stuff, and I didn't. But now, I've had a drink
– I drink!
I'm not afraid of anyone. Because I don't tell lies like
some people. . . Not even to myself.
Why should I be afraid of what people think? Scum of
the earth, that lot! "Look," I says, "I AM!"
A priest once said to me. . . He said to me, "The Devil
can boast better than anyone." You see, if you boast,
it's because you're scared of what people really think of
you. And if you're scared of what people really think,
you're dough in the Devil's hands. He can do with you
what he likes. Since I'm not afraid of people, it's easy
for me – Easy for me to spit in the Devil's beard. . .
And at his mother the old sow-features. So there!

NIKITA: *(Crossing himself.)* Then, what am I doing?

            Letting the rope drop.

MITRICH: What?

NIKITA: *(Gets down.)* You're saying I shouldn't be afraid of
            them?

MITRICH: Who? Those people? Don't let people frighten you.
            They're the scum of the earth. You only have to look at
            them in the bath house to see that they're all moulded
            of the same dough. One has a fat tummy, the other's
            thin, that's the only difference. Why be frightened of
            them? To hell with everybody!

MATRIONA: *(Coming out of the house.)* Are you coming?

NIKITA: I must go. I'm coming.

            Exit.

SCENE TWO

The same cottage as in Act One. The room is full of people. Some sitting, some standing. In the foreground Akulina and the Bridegroom. On one of the tables, an icon and some bread. The guests include Marina and her husband, and the village Policeman. The women are singing. Anisya is passing around the drink. The singing subsides.

COACHMAN: If we're going, let's go. It'll take us time to get to the church.

BEST MAN: Wait. We must wait. Her stepfather must give his blessing. Where is he?

ANISYA: He's on his way. Dear friends, he's coming. Fill your glasses. I want to see no one with an empty glass.

MATCHMAKER: Why's it taking him so long? He's kept us all waiting.

ANISYA: He's coming, he's coming. He'll be here before a girl has time to plait her hair. . . No matter how short. More drink everybody! *(Passing around the wine.)* He's coming, he's coming. Keep singing, my pretty ones! Keep singing till he arrives.

COACHMAN: They've waited so long, they've sung every song they know.

> *The women sing. Nikita and Akim enter during the song.*

NIKITA: *(Holding his father's arm. He pushes him into the room first.)* You go first, Papa. I can't do this without your help.

AKIM: I don't like to . . . I mean –

NIKITA: *(To the singers.)* Please. No more. *(Looking around the room.)* Is Marina here?

MATCHMAKER: Come on now, just pick up the icon, and give your blessing!

NIKITA: Wait. In a moment – *(He looks around the room.)* Is Akulina here?

MATCHMAKER: What is this? Roll call? Where else would she be? What a strange man.

ANISYA: What are you doing? Where are your boots?

NIKITA: Papa? Yes, good, you're here. Look at me! Everyone, look at me! You are all Christians – I kneel before you –

            Falls to his knees.

ANISYA: Darling Nikita, what's the matter? O – oh dear, my poor head!

MATCHMAKER: What's going on?

MATRIONA: I must apologise. Dear friends, he's had a bit too much of that French wine. Nikita, pull yourself together.

            She tries to lift him. He pays no attention to anyone, but stares straight ahead.

NIKITA: Fellow Christians, forgive me, for I have sinned. I must make my confession.

MATRIONA: *(Tugging at his shoulders.)* You're out of your mind! Dear friends, he's gone mad. Somebody help me take him away!

NIKITA: *(Shaking her off.)* Leave me alone! Papa, are you listening? First of all – Marina, please look at me. *(He bows to her and rises.)* I have sinned against you. I seduced you, deceived you, abandoned you. For Christ's sake, forgive me.

            Bows again.

ANISYA: What are you talking about? Nobody asked you to speak. Get up! This is obscene! What's the matter with you?

MATRIONA: O – oh he's bewitched. What's happening? He's gone mad. Get up! Get up! What is this nonsense?

            Pulling him.

NIKITA: *(Shaking his head.)* Leave me alone. Forgive me, Marina, for I have sinned against you. Forgive me for the sake of Jesus Christ our Lord.

            Marina puts her face in her hands. She is silent.

ANISYA: Get up! Did you hear what I said? GET UP! What's all the fuss about? What's past is past. Stop making a spectacle of yourself. Oh dear! He's gone completely mad!

NIKITA: *(Pushing his wife aside, he turns to Akulina.)* And you Akulina? I confess to you. Fellow Christians, I am a condemned man. Akulina, I have sinned against you. Your father didn't die a natural death. . . He was poisoned.

ANISYA: *(Screams)* Oh no, what's he saying?

MATRIONA: He's raving mad! Somebody take him away!

People step forward to take hold of Nikita.

AKIM: *(Stopping them.)* Wait. You must wait. Please listen to him. . . Wait, I'm telling you.

NIKITA: Akulina, I poisoned him. Forgive me in the name of Jesus Christ our Lord.

AKULINA: *(Jumps up.)* He's lying! I'm telling you, he's lying! I know who did it!

MATCHMAKER: Sit down! Who asked you to speak?

AKIM: O Lord. . . Sin upon sin.

POLICEMAN: Seize him! Send for the village elder! We'll need witnesses. Nobody leave. I must draw up an indictment.

AKIM: You, you . . . with the bright buttons. . . Wait! I say, WAIT! Just wait! Let him have his say.

POLICEMAN: Stay out of this old man. I must have a formal statement.

AKIM: I know. . . I understand. . . But please, don't talk to me about indictments, formal statements . . . whatever. This is God's work. This man is making his confession to God . . . and there you are talking about statements . . . and indictments –

POLICEMAN: Quickly, someone fetch the village elder.

AKIM: Please, he must be allowed to confess to God. Then by all means . . . by all means do whatever it is you have to do. He's not going to run away.

NIKITA: Akulina, I am guilty of another sin. I seduced you.
               Forgive me, in the name of Christ.

               He bows

AKULINA: *(Coming from behind a table.)* Leave me alone! I won't
               get married! You told me to! But I won't! I won't!

POLICEMAN: Now, would you mind repeating all you've said.

NIKITA: Please, let me finish first.

AKIM: *(In raptures.)* Speak child . . . Speak. Tell all there is to
               tell. Confess everything to God. Don't let people
               frighten you. Our Lord knows . . . knows everything
               . . .

NIKITA: I poisoned the father; ruined the daughter. I used my
               position to abuse her and kill our child –

AKULINA: It's true! It's true!

NIKITA: I smothered the baby. I dug a hole in the cellar. In the
               corner where the ground is soft. I placed that little
               body in the earth. I put a board across; and sat on that
               board. I sat there – crushed . . . crushed it! The baby's
               frail bones cracked under me. Then I covered the flat
               shape in soft damp earth. I did it. Me. On my own.

AKULINA: He's lying. I told him to.

NIKITA: No Akulina, don't try to protect me. I'm not afraid.
               Fellow Christians, forgive me! Forgive me!

               Bows.

               Silence.

POLICEMAN: Bind him. There can be no marriage –

               Men approach Nikita with their belts.

NIKITA: Wait! I'm not going to run away. *(Bows to his father.)*
               Papa forgive me. Forgive me. I am a poor sinner. You
               warned me. You used to say, "If a claw is caught, the
               bird is lost." But I didn't listen to you. Everything you
               said has come true. Forgive me in the name of Christ.

AKIM: My dear child, God will forgive you. *(Hugs Nikita.)*
               You've shown no mercy on yourself. Our Lord will

have mercy on you. This is His work. He will have mercy –

ELDER: *(Enters)* Good, there are plenty of witnesses –

POLICEMAN: We'll start the cross-examination immediately.

Nikita is bound hand and foot.

AKULINA: *(Goes to stand beside Nikita.)* I'll tell the truth. You can ask me anything you want.

NIKITA: There's no point asking questions. I'm responsible for everything that happened. I planned it all. I did it all. I've nothing more to say.

THE END

ALTERNATIVE ENDING TO ACT FOUR

SCENE TWO

The Cottage, the same as Act One. Anyutka, undressed, lying on a bench under a large coat. Mitrich is sitting on a bunk, smoking.

MITRICH: They've stunk the place out! Pah! To hell with them. They've spilt the drink everywhere. Even this tobacco can't get rid of the smell. The smell haunts me. O Lord! I'd better go to bed.

Is about to turn out the lamp.

ANYUTKA: *(Sits up with a start.)* Grandpa, don't turn it out!

MITRICH: Why not?

ANYUTKA: They're still out there in the yard. They're doing something – *(Listens)* Can you hear them? They've gone back into the barn.

MITRICH: Whatever it is they're doing, it's got nothing to do with you. If they wanted you to know, they would have said something. Now, lie down and go to sleep. I'll turn out the light!

Turning down the lamp.

ANYUTKA: No, please, Grandpa! Don't turn it down completely. Leave a little bit, a mouse eye, or I'll be too frightened.

MITRICH: *(Laughs)* All right, all right. Why are you frightened?

ANYUTKA: I can't help it, Grandpa. My sister was in such agony. She kept pounding her head on the chest. *(Whispers)* I know – I know she's going to have a baby. . . Maybe it's already born . . .

MITRICH: You little fly, you're too curious for your own good. The frogs will get you. Lie down and go to sleep. *(Anyutka lies down.)* That's a good girl. *(Covers her up.)* That's the way. If you know too much, you'll grow old too soon.

ANYUTKA: Will you sleep on the stove?

MITRICH: Where else? You're being silly now. Where else would I sleep? *(Covers her.)* Now just lie down and go to sleep.

Gets up and goes to the stove.

ANYUTKA: I heard it cry. Just one cry. I can't hear it now.

MITRICH: O Lord, Blessed St Nicholas! What can't you hear?

ANYUTKA: The baby.

MITRICH: There's no baby, that's why you can't hear it.

ANYUTKA: But I heard it. I promise you, I heard it. A little thin
            cry.

MITRICH: That's what you heard, eh? What you heard was the
            child snatcher. He had just popped a naughty little girl
            like you into his sack. Now he'll take her away.

ANYUTKA: What child snatcher?

MITRICH: The child snatcher. *(Climbing on to the stove.)* Ah, this
            stove is nice and warm now. Lovely! Oh Lord! Blessed
            St Nicholas!

ANYUTKA: Grandpa! Are you going to sleep?

MITRICH: What else would I be going to do? Sing songs?

ANYUTKA: Grandpa! Grandpa! They're digging. Honest to God,
            they're digging in the cellar. Listen! I promise you,
            they're digging!

MITRICH: Now what are you dreaming about? Don't be silly.
            Digging, at night? Who digs at night? It's the cow,
            having a good scratch. Digging? I'm telling you, go to
            sleep, or I'll turn the light out.

ANYUTKA: No, Grandpa, please, don't turn the light out. I won't
            say another word. I promise. I'll stop. But I'm so
            frightened.

MITRICH: Frightened? If you keep saying you're frightened,
            something will come and frighten you for real. Don't
            say it, don't even think it, and you'll be all right.
            You're a silly little girl.

Silence. The cricket chirps.

ANYUTKA: *(Whispers)* Grandpa! Hey, Grandpa! Are you asleep?

MITRICH: What's the matter, now?

ANYUTKA: What's he like, the child snatcher?

MITRICH: You want to know what he's like? Well, when there's
            somebody who won't go to sleep – let's say a little girl
            like you – well, he creeps along with his sack, finds the
            child; snatches her with the speed of a frog's tongue;
            puts her in the sack. Then he pops his own head in the
            sack. He lifts up her dress and he beats her.

ANYUTKA: What with?

MITRICH: Birch!

ANYUTKA: But if he's got his head in the sack, how can he see?

MITRICH: He can see all right.

ANYUTKA: I'd bite him.

MITRICH: No, you wouldn't be able to.

ANYUTKA: Yes I would. Grandpa, there's someone coming. Who
            is it? Holy Mother of God! Who is it?

MITRICH: Whoever it is, let them come! What's the matter with
            you? Here, I think it's your mother.

ANISYA: *(Enters)* Anyutka! *(Anyutka pretends she's asleep.)*
            Mitrich!

MITRICH: What?

ANISYA: Why's the lamp still on? We'll sleep in the summer
            wing.

MITRICH: I've only just finished working. I'll turn it out.

ANISYA: *(Searches through a chest, grumbling to herself.)* The one
            time you need it, it's nowhere to be found.

MITRICH: What you looking for?

ANISYA: I'm looking for my cross. I must lay it on him.
            Without the cross, he'll die unchristened. Lord have
            mercy! That'd be a sin!

MITRICH: Yes, yes. . . Well, you must do things properly. . .
            Well, have you found it?

ANISYA: I've found it. *(She leaves.)*

MITRICH: Just as well. Otherwise, I'd have to have given her mine. Oh Lord!

ANYUTKA: *(Sits bolt upright, trembling)* O – oh! Grandpa! Don't go to sleep! For Christ's sake! I'm so frightened!

MITRICH: Now, what's frightened you?

ANYUTKA: Will the baby die then? Grandma Matriona put a cross on Aunt Arina's baby – it died.

MITRICH: If it dies – They'll bury it.

ANYUTKA: Maybe it wouldn't have to die, if Grandma Matriona wasn't here. You see, I heard, I heard what Grandma said. I promise you, I heard it all.

MITRICH: What did you hear? I'm telling you, go to sleep. Pull that coat over your head, and you won't see or hear anything.

ANYUTKA: But if the baby's alive, I could nurse it.

MITRICH: *(Bellows)* O Lord!

ANYUTKA: Where will they put it?

MITRICH: They'll put it where it has to be put. In the proper place. It's none of our business. Go to sleep! Your mother will come, and she'll give it to you.

            Silence.

ANYUTKA: Grandpa, you know that girl you were telling me about the other day, well, did they kill her?

MITRICH: Which girl? The one I was telling you about? Oh, that girl. Everything turned out all right.

ANYUTKA: You'd just found her. What happened then? You found her and –

MITRICH: We found her.

ANYUTKA: But where was it? Tell me again!

MITRICH: We found her in what must have been her house. We soldiers arrived in this village; the villagers had all fled and we were just searching through the house when we found this little girl lying face down on the floor. They were going to pummel her head, but I felt sorry for her

and I took her in my arms. She fought tooth and nail
to be let go. She somehow seemed heavier than she
actually was. She grabbed hold of anything she could.
It was difficult to get her to let go. But I held her
tight.
Then I thought to stroke her head. I stroked her head,
as you would a little baby. Her hair was all bristly, like
a hedgehog's. I kept stroking her. . . I just stroked her,
and she eventually calmed down. I dunked a biscuit
and offered it to her. She nibbled at it. . . She liked it.
Now, what were we going to do with her? She was very
small. Well, we took her with us. We fed her, and fed
her, and she soon got used to us. We took her on the
march. She was with us all the time. She was a nice
little girl.

ANYUTKA: She wouldn't have been christened, would she?

MITRICH: Who knows? Unlikely. Her people were different from
us.

ANYUTKA: Were they Germans?

MITRICH: No. Not Germans, Asiatics. They're like Jews, but
they're not Jews. They're more like the Polish, but
they're Asiatics. They were called Kurgs or Kurds,
something like that, I've forgotten. We called the little
girl Sashka. Sashka was such a good little girl. You
know, I've forgotten almost everything, but that little
girl . . . Lord bless her . . . I can see her now. She's all
I can remember about my time in the army. No, I can
also remember how they used to beat me. I remember
the way Sashka used to cling to my neck when she was
being carried. You couldn't have found a better little
girl anywhere in the world. Eventually we had to give
her away. She was adopted by the sergeant's wife.
Everything turned out all right for her, in the end.
The soldiers were terribly sad to see her go.

ANYUTKA: Grandpa, I can remember when Papa died. You
weren't living with us then. He called for Nikita. This
was the day he died. And he said to him, "Forgive me,
Nikita", and then he started to cry. That was sad too.

MITRICH: Just the way things go, eh?

ANYUTKA: Grandpa, Grandpa! They're making a noise in the
            cellar again. O Mother of God, and all the Holy Saints!
            Oh Grandpa, I know they'll do something terrible to
            that baby. They'll kill it. But it'll be so small – O-oh!

            Covers her head and cries.

MITRICH: Yes my child, they're up to something terrible down
            there. Damn them. These women are vile creatures.
            Peasant men are bad enough, but the women, they're
            worse, they're like wild animals. There's nothing they
            won't do.

ANYUTKA: Grandpa! *(Gets up.)* Hey Grandpa!

MITRICH: What now?

ANYUTKA: The other day, there was this traveller who stayed the
            night. He said that when a child dies, its soul goes
            straight to heaven. Is that true?

MITRICH: How should I know? Yes. . . Probably. So?

ANYUTKA: Well, if it's true, I'd like to die now.

MITRICH: If you die, you're just another one off their list.

ANYUTKA: You're a child until you're ten. So my soul will still go
            to God. After I'm ten, my soul will no longer be
            innocent.

MITRICH: That's right, your soul will be tarnished. Your soul will
            be spoiled. But how can you women avoid being
            spoiled? No one teaches you anything. All that you see,
            and all that you hear, is evil. Nothing but evil. I may
            not be very clever, but I know what I know, and I
            know more than any peasant village woman. A woman,
            I ask you, what is she? Mud! There are millions of you
            in Russia. And you're all like moles – blind and
            ignorant. All you women know how to do is to cast
            your spells: You'll protect your plague-ridden cattle
            with a plough; you'll cure your children by putting
            them under the hen roost. That's all you know how to
            do.

ANYUTKA: Mama used to do that.

MITRICH: Well there you are. There are millions of you. Wild beasts of the forest. You grow up that way, and that's the way you are till you die! You see nothing: Hear nothing. But a man – in a tavern, or in prison, without ever meaning to – or in the army like me, he learns something about life. You can't ask a woman about God, about what's right and what's wrong. She won't know what's special about Fridays, Friday, Good Friday even. She just won't know anything about anything. Women, they crawl around like blind pups sniffing shit. Oh they sing their songs, "Ho, ho, ho", but they don't know what the "Ho, ho, ho", means.

ANYUTKA: But Grandpa, I know half the Our Father –

MITRICH: Good for you. But I'll never expect you to know it all, because who'll teach it you? Now and then a drunken peasant will beat you with his belt. I don't know what that'll teach you, but it's all the teaching you're going to get. When they put a sergeant in charge of recruits, he is responsible for them. But no one's responsible for the women in this country. You're like a herd of cattle with no herdsman – just running wild! You're the most ignorant creatures on this earth. You're just hopeless.

ANYUTKA: What am I going to do?

MITRICH: There's nothing you can do. Cover yourself up, and go to sleep!

Silence. The cricket chirps.

ANYUTKA: *(Starts)* Grandpa! Somebody's shouting! They're yelling something! Honest to God, he's shouting! Grandpa, he's coming here.

MITRICH: Pretend you're asleep.

Enter Matriona and Nikita.

NIKITA: What have they done to me? What've you done to me?

MATRIONA: You must have a drink. Here, have something to drink. *(Puts the drink in front of him.)* Now what's the matter?

NIKITA: Give it here. What if I don't?

MATRIONA: Shh! Not everyone's asleep you know. Come on, have something to drink!

NIKITA: What's happening! Why did we have to do that? Why didn't you just take it away?

MATRIONA: *(Whispers)* Sit down, will you? Sit down, here. And then have another drink, and something to smoke. It'll take your mind off it. You'll soon feel better.

NIKITA: Mama, dear Mama! I can't live any more. When it wailed, and I heard those little bones crack . . . krr . . . krr . . . krr . . . I couldn't bear it! I can't bear it!

MATRIONA: E – eh! What a lot of rubbish you talk. You've always been scared of the dark. Is that it? You're just a little scared of the dark. Well, when day breaks you'll feel better. A day or two will pass, and you'll forget.

             Puts her hand on Nikita's shoulder.

NIKITA: Keep away from me! What have you done to me?

MATRIONA: My child, what d'you mean?

             Taking him by the hand.

NIKITA: Just keep away from me! I'll kill you! I don't care any more! I'll kill you!

MATRIONA: There, there. . . You're scared. Why don't you go to bed?

NIKITA: There's nowhere I can go. I'm lost.

MATRIONA: *(Shaking her head.)* Oh dear, I'd better go and finish the job. He can sit here until he comes to his senses.

             She leaves.

NIKITA: *(Sits, his head in his hands. Mitrich and Anyutka are terrified.)* It's crying. . . It's true. . . It's crying. . . There. . . There. . . She'll bury it alive! She'll bury it alive! *(Rushes to the door.)* Mama, don't bury it! It's alive!

MATRIONA: *(Returns. Whispers.)* What are you talking about? Christ have mercy on you! Your imagination is playing tricks with you! How can it possibly be alive? You've crushed every bone in its body.

NIKITA: I'd like a drink.

             Drinks.

MATRIONA: My son, you must go now. . . Go to bed. . . To
            sleep. . . Sleep will do you good. . . It'll all be all right,
            you'll see.

NIKITA: *(Just stands there, listening.)* It's still alive! Listen! It's
            wailing! Can't you hear it? Listen!

MATRIONA: *(Whispers)* There's nothing there.

NIKITA: Dear Mama! My life's ruined. What have you done to
            me? Where shall I go?

            Rushes out of the house. Matriona follows.

ANYUTKA: Grandpa, did they strangle the baby?

MITRICH: *(Angry)* Go to sleep, can't you. Damn you, just go to
            sleep, before I hit you with the broom.

ANYUTKA: They did, didn't they?

MITRICH: Shh! Go to sleep!

ANYUTKA: Dearest Grandpa! There's something grabbing at my
            shoulders. It's got me with its claws. Scratching!
            Snatching! Grandpa, it's true, I promise. It's going to
            take me away. Grandpa, let me up on the stove with
            you. For Christ's sake, let me! It's got hold of me!
            Ahhh! *(Rushing to the stove and climbing on to it.)* You
            won't go away, will you? You'll stay all night?

MITRICH: Where else is there for me to go? Come on, climb up!
            Oh Lord, Blessed St Nicholas the Martyr, Holy Virgin
            Mother of Kazan! They've frightened the living
            daylights out of this child! You little fool. . . You little
            fool. . . It's true, those nasty women, they're very
            frightening. But don't let them frighten you. Good luck
            to them!